UNAUTHORIZED
Mouse Pin Trading Guide

The Beginner's Guide to the Fun and Exciting World of Disney Pin Trading!

Updated for
2016

By MousePinTrading.com

ISBN-13: 978-1537006031
ISBN-10: 1537006037

Legal Stuff

Dedication

This book is dedicated to the Disney Cast Members who work every day (and point with 2 fingers) to make us believe that the world can still be a magical place, to the Disney Pin Traders who pass on their knowledge, experience, and love of all things Disney, and to our families who share our love, our joy, and YES... even though they may not always admit it... our obsession!

"If you can dream it, you can do it..."

- Walt Disney

Acknowledgements

Mouse Pin Trading would like to acknowledge the generations of Pin Traders who have tirelessly posted, blogged, tweeted, pinned, and posted to various social media platforms to share their knowledge of Disney Pin Trading. Like almost everyone else out there, once we got the Pin Trading bug, we went hunting for more information.

Sites like OfficialDisneyPins.com, PinPics.com, and others contributed to our education and we would like to thank them for fueling our Pin Trading obsession.

We would also like to thank our families for their ongoing support and always constructive input!

About This Book

When we were putting this book together, there was one thing about Pin Trading we didn't know... YOU!

We didn't know if you were a seasoned trader looking for more info or a newbie who was just getting ready to trade your first pin, so we stuck a Hidden Mickey pin in the board and decided to give you everything. Just like pin trading, this book is an exploration of what we like to call "'Pin'formation!"

Pins + Information = `Pin'formation!

How can we explain that a bit better? You know how when you're walking down Main Street, you notice a few things at once. You notice how Main Street flows and makes sense. If you want to find something specific, it's right where you think it should be. At the same time, you notice how cool details are tucked away in the corners so if you want to meander your way through the alleys and shops, and explore the nooks and crannies, you discover amazing details... well, it's the same with this book!

The information included in this book flows so it's easy to find, but at the same time, we tucked juicy bits of "pin-formation" in between the checklists, resources, and detail. We've even included handy Mouse Pin Trading Tips which contain nuggets of Disney Pin Trading expertise and are highlighted with a Sorcerer Mickey so they are easy to spot.

So how you use this book is up to you...

You can bolt straight to the Checklists and Glossary for specific 'pin'formation, or pick a page and check out the pins and those Mouse Pin Trading Tips! Oh, by the way, all the pictures used in the book are pictures of actual Disney Trading Pins from our collections.

Always a work in progress...

This is the fifth edition of The Mouse Pin Trading Guide and we've expanded the Hidden Mickey Checklist, Pin Series Checklists and Glossary Sections. Of course, we've tried to include every tidbit of new 'Pin'formation that we've uncovered since we released the original guide, but you know Disney... they like to keep things moving! So...

What we couldn't jam into the book, or any new information that becomes available since publication, we post on our Facebook page which is located at Facebook.com/MousePinTrading. Make sure you "Like" us and share your pin trading experiences and expertise.

In the years since we launched the original book, we've been running into (and trading with) a growing number of people who are using the guide! It's our hope that this guide becomes an essential and fun tool in your Pin Trading Toolbox and that you refer to it often through every step of your Disney Pin Trading journey...

Now, let's get trading!

Contents

The Tale of the Pin...

Welcome to the amazing and occasionally obsessive world of Disney Pin Trading!

Pin Trading at Disney Parks is a fun and interactive way to interact with Disney Cast Members and other Disney Guests while discovering cool and sometimes valuable pins along the way, and it's open to anyone over the age of 3! All it takes is a few pins, a lanyard and a desire to expand your Disney Park experience! Pixie Dust is optional, but always good to have on hand...

This guide is compiled from our families' personal pin trading experiences in Disneyland and Walt Disney World. We felt it would be a great idea to share our experience in Pin Trading as we have definitely seen what works and what can cost you a ton of money and frustration. By sharing our experience, we hope that this guide will assist you on your Pin Trading Adventures and help to map out a few exciting points of interest along the way.

You don't have to be a serious Pin Trader to have a great Disney Pin Trading experience. In fact, the whole program is designed for all Disney guests, from the folks on their first visit, to the Annual Pass Holders who are in the park every week. It's a great way to meet people, interact and talk about their favorite Disney Characters. We have met some amazing people through pin trading and it's a fantastic way to meet people from all over the world with one thing in common –

they all love Disney! In fact, "Excuse me… may I please see your pins?" might be the best icebreaker line, ever!

Mouse Pin Trading Tip!

Most Cast Members are also Pin Traders, so they have a wealth of knowledge. When you have some downtime in your day, ask them what they collect. You never know where the conversation may lead. There is a Cast Member who works Custodial (the folks who keep everything bright and shiny) in Downtown Disney named Tom. The first time we met him, we traded pins and then chatted for a few minutes. The next day, he had several pins that my kids had been looking for, and the next day, and the day after that. Tom still worked there the last time we were in Disneyland® and every time we see him, he pulls out his bag of pins.

Ready for the amazing part? To this day, he remembers all of our favorite Disney Characters!

Our family first got interested in Disney pins during our very first visit to Disneyland when our son and daughter were 7 and 9. We have been back to a Disney Park at least twice a year since that first visit, and pin trading has become a main ingredient for a memorable trip. When it comes to Disney Pin Trading, we need to make sure we maximize our time in the park because it's not like we will be back next week to complete a pin set (we actually live in Vancouver, BC). We found that most of the pin traders we were meeting were Local Resident Annual Pass Holders who were in the park every Thursday when the new pins come out, so most of their advice, although interesting, was not of any use to us as we didn't know when we would be back!

It's great that if you live in Southern California or Orlando you can pop into the park whenever a cool pin is being released, but for us regular vacation types, what can we do?

Well, using the information we are going to share with you in this guide, my family has been able to trade an average of 300 – 400 pins in a 3-5 day visit to the park… and go on all our favorite attractions… and get 40 or more Disney Character Signatures, all with just a little planning and insight.

Like I said, we know how to maximize our time at Disney!

When you really dive into Disney Pin Trading, there is a lot of information to digest. We will do our best to simplify as much as possible and make sure you have the Pin Trading lingo you need to enjoy your experience without becoming overwhelmed.

So, in the words of that eternal Lost Boy, Peter Pan… "HERE WE Gooooooo!"

Occasionally... Disney comes out with a set or series of pins that is complete by itself, and then later releases a complimentary set that makes it even better. In 2010, the Pin with Purchase (PWP) series was a set of keys that were made to look like different Disney Characters. Then in 2013, they releases a Pin with Purchase (PWP) series that was the corresponding locks for those keys. Each set was great by itself, but put them together and it is an even better collection. Of course this also keeps you looking *for just one more pin!*

2010 Pin with Purchase Key Set

2013 Pin with Purchase Lock Set

How Did We Get Started?

Confessions of a Disney Pin Addict

The first time we took the family to Disneyland, we knew we were going to "Go Big", so we budgeted for everything... or so we thought. We budgeted for the Character Breakfast and Dinners, lots of Souvenirs, a "Discover the Magic Tour"... we even had a Turkey Leg and Pickle budget! What we didn't account for were all these really cool lanyards covered with bright shiny Disney pins that everyone was wearing... and they were trading other bright shiny pins with Disney Cast Members!

We had to get in on the action!

So we ran to the nearest store (fortunately there is a shopping opportunity every 20 feet or so in any Disney Park) and asked how to get started. A very helpful Cast Member (who was wearing a lanyard full of princess pins that my daughter wanted to trade for) walked us over to the Pin Section and we were on our way.

Our first Pin Trading bill read like this:

Tinkerbell Starter Set with Lanyard:	$44.95
Sorcerer Mickey Lanyard Starter Set:	$44.95
Regular Adult Lanyard:	$8.95
Tinkerbell Lanyard Medallion:	$9.95
Sorcerer Mickey Lanyard Medallion:	$9.95
4 Pin Starter Set:	$22.95
Total (not including taxes):	$141.70

By the way, that sound you hear is our budget flying away to Neverland... but we're good to go, right? Not so much. You see, being good parents, we were foolish enough to spend a lot of time pointing out all the really cool pins and pin sets, so when it came to trading, neither of our children wanted to trade their pins! They didn't even want to trade the duplicates on the lanyard set!

So... back to the pin rack to pick out the ugliest pins we could find. Add to the tab:

4 Pin Starter Set #2:	$22.95
4 Pin Starter Set #3:	$22.95
Total (not including taxes):	$44.90
That puts the running total at:	**$187.60**

Now we're all set! We have pins, our lanyards are bright and shiny and we are surrounded by smiling Cast Members who let us know that we can each trade up to 2 pins with them per day. Perfect!

Our inventory of trading pins lasted exactly 16 minutes.

Fortunately, we hadn't even managed to make our way out of the store yet, so the pin rack was close by! We frantically started looking through each box of starter pins looking for the best deal (now thinking on a cost per pin basis) and found out that the magic of Disney also extended to their pricing strategy!

Every pin set worked out to $4.27 per pin or more, when we looked at packs with 7 pins in the set (4 pin sets worked out to an even higher price per pin). Let's face it, the people behind the Mouse know how to create a magical experience in the park and at the cash register as your purchases magically add up!

To make a long cash register receipt short, by the end of our first day in Disneyland, we had purchased and traded a total of 72 pins. The price tag for our new addiction (including lanyards and a few Limited Edition Pins) was $544.00 USD (not including tax, of course) and the receipts stacked higher than the Matterhorn! That, combined with the "what happened to the budget?" look on my wife's face should have been the last chapter of our Disney Pin story, but we were hooked.

We spread our lanyards and the pins that would not fit on the lanyards out on the bed and basked in their shiny brilliance. We spent the next hour examining our booty and sorting each pin by character. Our son was collecting Sorcerer Mickey and Stitch Pins. Our daughter was collecting Tinkerbell and Princess Pins and my wife (despite the disapproving look on her face) had managed to gather a sizeable Eeyore collection. Even though Dad (that's me) was mainly responsible for inventory (running back and forth between the store and my family) and didn't have a lanyard of my own, there were still a good number of Grumpy Pins that were collected on my behalf! Hint taken.

All was going well... and then our daughter noticed a small Mickey Head on one of her Tink pins... and then another... and another! We picked one up, turned it over and read those words that forever changed our Pin Trading world:

"Cast Lanyard Collection" – "Pin 2 of 10"

There were other collections hidden amongst our new found pins! We knew we had no choice but to complete these Hidden Mickey collections... and that would require more traders.

Fortunately for us, The World of Disney Store was open until midnight and within walking distance of the hotel, so we could stock up before we got to the park in the morning and not waste a moment of trading time!

By the end of our first Disney vacation, we had spent over $1,200.00 in pins, completed the entire Cast Lanyard Series for that year, plus more than half of the previous year's collection and our suitcases were heavier by about 6 pounds.

We travelled back to Vancouver, already discussing what type of pins would be out at Christmas and planning our next trip to The Happiest Place on Earth... and then I looked at the expression on Mom's face. We knew from that expression that if we wanted to keep up our newly found obsession, we needed to find a way to make it more cost effective. Adding $1,200.00 to the Disney budget for trading pins wasn't going to fly no matter how much Pixie Dust we threw at it! As it stood, our new obsession with Disney Pins could actually squash our chances of ever coming back, if we didn't find an economical solution.

Mouse Pin Trading Tip!

Note to Moms: She was right of course...

Spending thousands of dollars on pins was out of the question, and if you plan on Pin Trading as part of your Disney Trip you need to have a budget. Let me rephrase that: Your family is going to want to trade pins and even if your children are too young to trade themselves, then you are going to want to collect for them! Pin Trading is part of the Disney Experience and an amazing way to meet people. Again, if your experience is anything like ours, they are going to want to trade pins, so have the discussion and plan for it, so you don't have a "Non-magical Moment" in the middle of Main Street!

Don't get me wrong, we had an absolute blast trading almost 200 pins, met some great people and had some amazing conversations, but reality kicks in when you have to pay the Visa bill, so it was time to correct and continue - Christmas was only 10 months away!

We needed a plan, and to build that plan we needed information. So we started to dig.

We started our Disney Pin Education by finding out just how many types of Disney Pins there were to trade, and to be traded. We were amazed to find that there are over 90,000 pins (now all these years later, it is more like 116,000 pins) out there! We found that the more familiar we were with what was out there, the better we were at making trades and talking to other pin traders. We had to look in a lot of places and deal with a lot of conflicting information, but after we sorted through the mish-mash we had a pretty clear idea of what was out there.

Here's what we found...

It All Started with a Mouse... Pin.

Collectible pins have always been part of the Disney experience, but Pin Trading officially started in Walt Disney World in 1999 during the Millennium Celebration, spreading to Disneyland California the following year. Since then, well over 116,000 pins have been released by Disney in various editions and collections. Pins that were released exclusively in one park will say on the back which Disney Park it came from, including Paris, Tokyo and Hong Kong. Each resort has their own exclusive pins and as Disney expands resort locations across the globe, like the Aulani Resort in Hawaii and the brand new Shanghai Disneyland, we can expect to see more exciting pins on the horizon. To help you sort through the smorgasbord of Disney pins, here is a quick description of the types of pins that Disney produces...

❖ **Cast Lanyard or Hidden Mickey Pins** are only available by trading with Cast Members or in Mystery Packs. (see Tip below) The Hidden Mickey pins have a small Mickey Mouse silhouette hidden somewhere on the face of the pin and began showing up in Disney Parks in 2005. Before that were the Cast Lanyard Pins. These were also only available through Cast Members but did not have a Mickey symbol on the front. Disney added the Mickey symbol to make the pins more recognizable... and who doesn't like finding a Hidden Mickey!

These are the pins that moved my family from casual hobby to obsession. As these pins can only be traded for and are not available for purchase, the only way to get them is to be in the park when they are released. The pins are released in waves and there will be different collections in each park, so it may be difficult to collect an entire series during one visit. Also, the pins don't always all come out at once. Disney will stagger the release and limit the amount of pins given out. The first wave of the annual HM series is usually released in January, with Wave 2 usually released in September. Completer Pins for the series can be released at any time during the year, but most often show up later in the year. Hidden Mickey Pins are distributed by Cast Members who, at the start of their shift, load up their pin lanyards and venture out in the park to do their jobs and extend the pin trading experience with Disney Guests, and these coveted pins are tucked away on those lanyards. Some of these pins are exclusive to one park, while others are part of the Global Lanyard Series and will be released across all Disney parks. The Hidden Mickey Checklists can be found at the back of this Guide.

❖ **Chaser Pins** are pins that look like Disney forgot to apply the enamel finish! In other words, they are plain metal. Chasers can be either Silver or Gold and are becoming a very popular edition to the Hidden Mickey and Mystery Pin Series. The 2011 Hidden Mickey Series saw a 20 pin Chaser set that had pin traders running around trying to figure out what pins were in the series. To complicate things, 2 of the Chaser pins were the same pin (Square Figment) with different series numbers and one pin Chaser pin was actually released in color! Like we said, Disney likes to keep us guessing! Chasers do not have a separate designation on the pin back, but they are usually numbered separately from the original series.

Mouse Pin Trading Tip!

Mystery Packs: At various stores within the parks you can purchase Mystery Packs of Hidden Mickey Pins. The individual pins in the packs are wrapped in cardboard so you usually can't feel what they are, but you never know it is worth giving it a quick try.

Completer pins are offered the same way, so you can try asking a knowledgeable Cast Member if they have an idea which types of pins are in which colored packs.

❖ **Completer Pins** are Disney's way to keep you guessing! Just when you think you've completed a series, you find out there is one more pin. Disney creates a special pin that "Completes" a Hidden Mickey, Special Edition and Gift with Purchase pin series. The Hidden Mickey Completers are found on the Cast Member Lanyards like the regular HM pins, or in mystery bags, and the GWP pins are randomly placed within the purchase selection. The Special Edition Completer Pins are usually available only at special events. These pins will have

"Completer Pin" stamped on the pin back. Some pin sets will have more than one completer and there may be a different completer pin for each park. There are also Completer pins exclusive to high end series and framed pin sets. If you want these very exclusive pins, be prepared to shell out big bucks or do some very impressive trading!

❖ **Gift with Purchase Pins (GWP)** can be purchased at specific Pin Stores in all parks for around $2.95 depending on the collection with a minimum purchase (usually around $30.00). These pins are also given out randomly, so you often

see them on Cast Member Lanyards. On a trip to WDW, we collected the entire postcard set on the first day we were in the park. GWP pins will be stamped "Gift with Purchase" or simply "GWP" on the back and usually be a numbered (1 of..., 2 of...) set. Some will simply say Limited Release. These sets change a couple of times per year and if you're purchasing merchandise in the parks it is a good way to get inexpensive pins to trade. These sets are fun to trade for as collectors are snapping them up and putting doubles on their trading lanyards. We've never purchased the GWP sets, yet we've collected 5 complete GWP series. You just need to keep your eyes open!

❖ **Rack or Open Edition Pins** are found on the racks in Disney retail shops. They range in price from $6.95 to $15.95 and the selection includes everything from your favorite Disney Character to your favorite Disney Attraction. My family will make a game of trading for rack pins by picking a few we like in the stores and then trying to find them on a lanyard. We do the same thing for pin sets, which are also considered Open Edition. It's amazing what you can find when you pay attention and can trade a pin you don't like for one that retails for $6.95 or more. Rack pins are color coded by price and style so you can fall in love with a pin before you realize its $15.95!

Mouse Pin Trading Tip!

As Disney releases new pins every week, keeping track of what pins are available and finding out how, where, and when they will be released can get complicated! When you register your book on our website, you can see all the new information that we have added since this edition came out, plus we are always posting the latest information on our website and in our Facebook group, so make sure that you connect with us.

MousePinTrading.com – Website
PinCollectorsSociety.com – Facebook Group

- ❖ **Limited Edition and Limited Release Pins** are just what they sound like. They are pins with a limited edition size of anywhere between 50 and 10,000 and can be a single pin or a pin set. The lower the number, the harder they are to find and the more valuable they are. Throughout the year, Disney will run Limited Release Events where guests are given the opportunity to purchase low edition pins based on a random selection process. Check the Disney Pin Trading site for details and events. Limited Editions will have the words LIMITED EDITION on the back stamp and also note the Edition Size.

- ❖ **Cast Member Exclusive Pins** are not to be confused with Cast Lanyard Pins. Cast Member exclusive pins can only be purchased by Cast Members, so they are rare to find in the parks. On top of this, there are also pins that are exclusive to different groups within Disney (IE: Disney Studio's and WDI, Imagineering) so keep an eye out for these extremely exclusive pins. These pins can be Open or Limited Edition and will often commemorate a special event (IE: Earth Day) Imagineering Pins have a Mickey Sorcerer Hat imprinted on the back. Each Cast group within Disney (IE: Laundry or Security) can have pins that are exclusive to that group, which makes these pins fun and special to collect.

❖ **Artist Proof Pins** will have a small "AP" on the back stamp. Note that AP can also stand for "Annual Passholder". Artist Proof Pins are rare, as they are the actual pins that were used by the artist in the development of the pin. Many of them never made it to mass production, but become available on the secondary market and at special

pin trading events. The value of an AP pin increases dramatically for some collectors when it is signed by the artist, who will happily sign their creations at special Pin Trading Nights!

❖ **Annual Passholder Pins** (AP) are available to guests who hold an Annual Pass for either Disneyland or Walt Disney World Parks. The pins are only available for the Park that the pass is valid for (IE: You can't buy Annual Passholder Pins in WDW if your pass is for Disneyland). All AP Pins are Limited Edition or Limited Release. Often a series of AP Pins will be released throughout the year, usually a pin a month or quarter. In recent years there has also been an Annual Passholder "set" that has a higher edition size and is available all year long. Each annual passholder may purchase up to 2 pins per annual pass. This policy isn't tracked very closely, so many annual passholders will purchase more than 2 pins by visiting different retail locations throughout the parks, but this behavior is in that big category of "frowned upon" so use your own judgement here...

Mouse Pin Trading Tip!

Annual Passholder Pins can only be purchased if you are a current Annual Passholder. This kind of stinks if you only visit the park once or twice a year and can't justify the cost of an annual pass. So what can you do? Talk to people! We have never failed to find someone who offers to use their annual pass to buy us a pin (we pay for it of course) as they are allowed to get 2 pins per pass. You might not feel comfortable asking, but if the opportunity comes up, take it.

❖ **Special and Exclusive Pins**

Disney loves to commemorate events and acknowledge achievement with pins, so there are a wide variety of pins that can only be found from certain Cast Members and even then by Cast Members who are willing to part with these special and emotionally charged pieces of Disneyana.

Mouse Pin Trading Tip!

Occasionally Pin Traders who represent the values of Disney Pin Trading get rewarded with one of these special pins that would normally be reserved for Cast Members. During a trip to the Magic Kingdom, my son was given a Top Dog Trader Pin for his patience, recognition of other traders, pin knowledge, and a firm handshake! It is now his favorite and most valued pin.

Special Event Pins are given out for attending exclusive engagements, tours, and activities at Disney. You could say that these pins are the most valuable pins to have because to get them you have to purchase the event ticket which usually comes with a

high price tag. How do you collect these pins without paying $75.00 - $250.00 per person??? TRADE FOR IT!

❖ **Cast Member Recognition Pins** are given to Cast Members who achieve milestone years of service and who are recognized for providing an exceptional guest experience. These pins can be specific to a division or group within Disney. For example Custodial and Laundry Services have some really cool pins that no one else can get.

Also, each division of WDC (the Walt Disney Companies) seems to have their own pin collections (WDI – Walt Disney Imagineering and WDBS – Walt Disney Burbank Studios would be two of these) and they can only be purchased or awarded to the Cast Members who work in that division and sometimes even at a specific location.

❖ **Seasonal Pins & Pin Sets** (All Parks and Groups) are released for pretty much everything you can think of! Of course the big holidays get the most attention, but you can also find pins to commemorate Friday the 13th, Earth Day and even National Hug Day! Most of these seasonal pins are Limited Release and Limited Edition and as they are associated with those times of year that we like to  give gifts, they tend to be highly collectible. These pins can also end up on the discount racks of the Outlet Stores after the dated holiday has passes, so they make pretty cool traders, and it can be fun to put 25 "Bosses Day 2008" Pins back into circulation in the park. Did I mention that Disney pins make great stocking stuffers? In fact, sometimes they are the stocking!

❖ **Exclusive Group Pins** (D23, Club 33, Disney Vacation Club, Disney Visa) are available only through exclusive membership clubs with Disney.

○ **D23 merchandise** can only be purchased by D23 Club Members (available to all guests through a paid subscription) and include

single pins and pin sets that are available to members only. Exclusive pins are also available at the annual D23 expo in Anaheim, CA. Additionally, there are travelling D23 Members Only events all over the world, and at some of them, they also have a "Pop-up Store" of merchandise from "Mickeys of Glendale".

○ **Disney Club 33 Pins** are a little tougher to get as they are only sold within Club 33, the exclusive, members only restaurant in Disneyland. If you know someone who is a member, then you may be able to swing an invite, but regardless only members can actually purchase and of the merchandise, so ask nicely!

○ **Disney Vacation Club & Disney Visa Pins** are available to members and cardholders only. You must show valid membership ID and matching photo ID at time of purchase. We're not here to plug vacations and credit cards, but there are definite advantages to being members. Besides the pins, Disney parks also set up exclusive character meet and greets and special events for members...

❖ **Disney Auction Pins** were sold online through disneyauctions.com until 2004. Also known as P.I.N.S or Purchase It Now Pins, which was the name of the of the online auction program, these pins pop up on the secondary market and can be identified by the "Gavel" imprint on the back and DISNEYAUCTIONS.COM on the back stamp. Most of these pins are low edition Limited Edition pins and, as they have not been available for some time, are highly sought after. Make sure you get the Disney Auction Pin Backer Board with your purchase.

❖ **Ghirardelli Soda Fountain and Chocolate Shop (GSF)** aka: **Disney Studio Store Hollywood (DSSH)**, aka **Disney Soda Fountain Shop (DSF)** – Anyone for ice cream?

The Disney Soda Fountain Shop was located on Hollywood Blvd in Hollywood, CA and I have to thank fellow Pin Trader, Erin, for introducing my family to DSF! The Soda Fountain has gone through many changes since we first stumbled onto this hidden Disney gem on Hollywood Boulevard in 2007. Back then, it was still called the Disney Soda Fountain Shop and Studio Store and almost no one seemed to know about it. Since then, it has become the setting for some of the most insane activity in Disney Pin Trading. It underwent a change of management in late 2013 and the ice cream portion of the shop is run by the same Ghirardelli's that has shops in both parks. The store portion is now called Disney Studio Store Hollywood (DSSH). The pins from DSSH (lets go with that for simplicity) are some of the most sought after items, mainly due to the high resale value. Collectors will line up all night for a chance at an LE DSSH pin and for many Pin Traders, it's just too intense.

DSSH pins are usually limited editions of 500 (recently 750) or less (usually 150 for Surprise Pins) including their Pin Trader Delight Pin which only comes with the Pin Trader Delight Sundae. New DSSH pins are released every month and these pins can be identified by the "Ice Cream Cone" imprint on the back. DSSH also has special movie event pins as the shop is attached to the El Capitan Theatre.

Like I said, when we wrote the first edition of the Mouse Pin Trading Guide, the Disney Soda Fountain was a little known pin resource. Now, the Limited Edition releases are some of the most sought after pins in the world of Disney Pin Collecting. The demand has been so great that The Soda Fountain Shop had to put a lottery process in place to avoid pin traders from lining up days in advance and camping out on Hollywood Blvd!

The Disney Studio Store Hollywood (DSSH) pins can be split into 6 categories:

1. **Limited Editions** of 150, 300, 400, 500, and 750 which include the Marquee Pin Series which feature the El Capitan Theatre Marquee sign. The El Capitan is an amazing place to see the latest Disney movie release and is attached to the Disney Soda Fountain Shop.

2. **Special Release Pins** – Exclusive to Pin Trading Events and highly sought after. These can include Surprise Release pins that have a low edition size and are not announced until the actual event or pin release day.

3. **Marquee Pins** – These pins depict the El Capitan Theatre Sign (Marquee) and are produced for each Disney movie release. DSSH also releases special marquee puzzle pins that can be put together to form a jumbo marquee. These sets can be from 9 to 12 pieces and retail for $8.95 -$12.95 each.

4. **Pin Trader Delight Pins** – A LE 300/400/500/750 gift with purchase pin that comes with the Pin Traders Delight Sundae. The sundae retails for about $17, but some of the pins are fetching over $200 on the secondary pin market.

5. **Disney Beloved Tales Pins** – Depicting your favorite Disney movies, the earlier releases of these pins can be worth hundreds of dollars on the secondary market. At the time of writing this, a Beauty & The Beast Beloved Tales Pin sold for $759.99 USD. Not bad considering the pins retail for around $14.95!

6. **Open Edition Pins** – These pins were introduced to the DSF line up in 2012 and can be found on the small pin racks in the merchandise section of the shop with any leftover Limited Edition pins... if there are any!

Okay, back to the limited edition pin releases. Like we said, folks used to camp out on Hollywood Blvd to get a shot at getting one or two of the limited edition pins, and this caused a few issues for obvious reasons... Hollywood Blvd at 3am on a Saturday morning is definitely not the Happiest Place on Earth!

In order to control the crowds and create a fair distribution system, DSSH introduced the lottery system. The system is not without fault, but it has made the distribution of pins a lot more civilized. The downside is that you may line up and not get a pin... like we said, it's a lottery and the pins are limited to 1 or 2 per voucher. Here's how it works, straight from the DSSH Facebook page

Pin Release on Saturday, July 30, 2016 at 8:00am

In the interest of hosting a safe, fair, and fun sales event for everyone, we will implement the following queuing plan for Saturday's release of our *Rattle Series* collectible pins.

Each style of pin is limited to one (1) per person, per day, ages four years and up.

- All guests in line **by 7:00 am Saturday** morning will receive a wristband which entitles them to participate in the voucher raffle.

- Guests must be in line to receive a wristband. We will not wristband guests who are not in the official line.

- At 7:15am, all wrist-banded guests in line will be handed a randomly drawn numbered voucher from a drum containing numbered vouchers equal to the number of guests in line. The number on the voucher becomes the guest's line position. Guests should enter in ascending voucher numerical order starting at 8:00am.

- **Pins are sold in voucher numerical order**, and guests **must be in line in voucher numerical order** when their number reaches the door, or they forfeit their voucher, and can rejoin the line at the end.
  - **Guests who have multiple vouchers in their group, must also pay in voucher order**.

- Vouchered guests #1-100 should line up in numerical order at the Studio Store front entrance.

- Vouchered guests #101-200 should be numerical order by 8:15am

- Vouchered guests #201-300 should be in numerical order by 8:45am.

- Vouchered guests #301-400 should be in numerical order by 9:15am.

- Vouchered guests #401-500 should be in numerical order by 9:45am.

- Vouchered guests #501-600 should be in numerical order by 10:15am.

- Pin Trader Delights will be sold during the release beginning at 8:00am. There will be two lines for vouchered guests, one for Numbers 1 and above purchasing *the Rattle Series* set and/or Pin Trader Delights. The second line will be for guests with numbers 301 & above who will be allowed to purchase Pin Trader Delights only. Pin Trader Delights will only be sold in **voucher order in each of the two lines**. After the release has concluded, Pin Trader Delights will be sold at its normal time beginning at store opening until 10pm. (2 sundaes per voucher, per person, per set).

- Restrooms in the store will be available for use beginning at 5:15am. Restrooms will close once the voucher raffle begins, and will re-open once the store opens for sales at 8:00am.

- Both wristbands (intact and not tampered with) and vouchers must be present at the time of purchase. Vouchers must be surrendered at the time of purchase. <u>One set per transaction per voucher. Transaction must be paid for by voucher holder.</u>

- Numbered vouchers for our pin releases may not be sold or offered for sale. Any numbered voucher(s) that have been sold or offered for sale will be deemed invalid and will not be accepted at our pin releases.

This process has changed several times so for the latest information please visit the Disney Soda Fountain Facebook page to make sure the process hasn't undergone another magical transformation!

OK, enough about DSSH, now back to the show (or list)…

- ❖ **Disney Resort Hotel Series pins** are released sporadically through Disney Resorts to guests of the resorts. These sets can contain 20 or more pins, so if you start to collect one of these sets, you need to bring your patience along. The pins will be marked "Disneyland (or WDW) Resort Hotel Series" on the back stamp. We haven't seen a new hotel series in a long while, but they do pop up on lanyards.

- ❖ **The Disney Store (DS)** pins are sold (of course) through the Disney Store, either online or in some (very few) of the physical retail locations throughout the world. As well as offering their own pins, The Disney Store also retails D23 Member Pins and Disney Park Pins through the online store.

At peak times throughout the year, DS will offer Mystery Box Sets which will contain Limited Edition Pins with an edition size from 25 – 5000. Check out their sale section (previously known as Disney Outlet) for pin deals. The UK has a separate site, and offers a unique line of pins. You can also look at www.disneystore.co.uk to see the UK collection. Both offer Theme Park Exclusive Pins, so if you don't live close to a Disney Park, you can still get them through the website! As of this update, the UK Disney Store will only ship to valid addresses within the UK.

You can also purchase Disney Pins on line through odpt.com (Official Disney Pin Trading) but it's a bit of a wonky process. You have to contact Disney Merchandise Guest Services at 407.363.6200 or send them an email at wdw.mail.order@disneyworld.com to place your order. You need to reference the SKU #, give a description of the pin and how many you want. Open Edition pins are available immediately after the release date and Limited Edition pins are available 30 days after they are released.

Mouse Pin Trading Tip!

Location Exclusives: Some locations, such as the Disney Store in Times Square, NY will offer exclusive pins that can really make great additions to your collection. Look for the NYC Stamp on the back of the pin to make sure it's an exclusive NYC Pin. Due to a name change back in 2012, some NYC items will say "World of Disney" and others will say "Disney Store NYC" on them, depending on when they were produced.

- ❖ **Disney Cruise Lines & Disney Adventures** both have pin collections that are unique to the experience. One of the most commonly asked questions we receive from our Facebook page is "Can you trade pins on a Disney Cruise?" The answer is a big happy YES! While Disney Adventure Pins are designed to commemorate your experience (not many Disney pin shops on Mt Kilimanjaro), Disney Cruise Lines have been  expanding the pin collection almost as fast as they've been expanding the fleet! Cast Members wear pin trading lanyards and they host special Pin Trading Evenings, so bring traders!

- ❖ **AAA, Disney Movie Club,** and even **Costco** all offer pins available for trading in the parks (as long as they say Disney on the back) and some of them are very cool. Like we said earlier, there are over 116,000 pins in the Disney Pin Collection and it grows every day of the year so we are sure you will run into a few we haven't mentioned. If you find a pin you aren't sure of, you can ask the group on the Disney Pin Trading Facebook page.

❖ **Vinylmation** – A growing trend in Disney collectibles are Vinylmation 3D Rubber figures, so it was just a matter of time before they made their way to the Disney Pin World. The first run of

Vinylmation pins were finished with cloisonné or hard enamel, but the later editions mimic the rubber that the actual figures are made of. Disney has produced pins with rubber features on them for a long time, but the Vinylmation pins have so much rubber on them that Disney had to amend

the Pin Trading Guidelines. The old rules state that the pins must be metal. The amended rules now state that a pin must have a metal back with the Disney Copyright to allow the Vinylmation pins to be traded, as the rubber front is fused to a metal back. This is so they will not be confused with the 100% rubber pins that have been produced in the past and are not tradable in Disney Parks.

❖ **Pins to Avoid:** Like anything that is good or popular, there is always a dark side. Just watch any Disney movie! For every Snow White, there is an Evil Queen, and the Evil Queen of the pin world is the Scrapper! Since we wrote the first edition of this book, Scrapper pins have flooded the market and eBay pages. If you are concerned about buying fake pins, then your best bet is always to buy directly from Disney locations. While we can't recommend any specific sellers, if you ask in the Facebook group, I'm sure that you will get some good pointers.

Scrappers are evil! When Disney Pins are produced, there are sometimes additional runs that get produced beyond the amount ordered by Disney. These are Black Market pins that are not authorized by Disney and may have subtle differences in color, size, detail or back stamp. Scrappers can be hard to spot, but as awareness of the fake pins increases so does the database of what to look out for.

The majority of Scrapper pins are in the Cast Lanyard Series so a good rule of thumb is that if the pin was released in Florida, but you see it in California on the day of release (or before!) it's probably a Scrapper, a good sign if you're on eBay, is if the pin is shipping direct from China, pass on it. Quite frankly, we've been told so many contradictory ways of identifying Scrappers that we just use the same rule we use for everything: If we like the pin and it looks legit, we trade for it. If it has rough edges, bubbles in the enamel or the color looks a bit off, we pass. You can do your part by not introducing these pins into the parks. *How you ask?* Only buy pins from reputable sellers and avoid buying from overseas where the pins are produced for Disney. Read the next few pages carefully for tips on avoiding and spotting fake pins.

DisneyAuctions.com

How to Spot a Scrapper (Fake) Pin

Scrappers have become a more serious issue for Disney Pin Traders and Collectors. This makes buying authentic Disney pins online a bit more complicated and has even prompted people to stop buying online at all to avoid buying fake pins.

We think that's a bit extreme and there are ways to make sure you are buying Authentic Disney Pins, which we cover in the "Where to Buy Your Pins" section of this book.

As we've said several times, the best way to guarantee that you are getting Authentic Disney Pins is to purchase your trading pins in a Disney Park or from an authorized Disney retailer. Unfortunately, that means you will also be paying a minimum of $4 per pin, which may put a damper on your Pin Trading budget! And even when you pay more for your pins, it doesn't guarantee that the pins you are trading for are authentic. The really ugly thing about Scrappers is that they cause doubt.

When you see that Holy Grail pin on a Cast Members lanyard, how do you know if it's real? We've included a few pointers to help you out.

Below you will find the illustrated guide (We call them the CSI's) to identify a Scrapper pin. But there are a common sense points that will also help:

1. If you see the same pin over and over again on Cast Member Lanyards, there is a good chance it's a fake as Scrappers come in the same designs. This means that everyone who bought their pins from nasty online scrapper sellers will have the same pins to trade. There are unscrupulous dealers who buy scrappers from overseas wholesalers and then hit the parks early in the morning to trade them for legitimate Disney pins. They then sell the legit pins online for a profit.

2. Ask Cast Members if the pin is from Walt Disney World or Disneyland and do your homework (IE: look in at the checklists in this book before you head

to the park to get familiar with the pins. If you really want to do your homework, go online and Google "Disney Pins Wholesale" and look at the lists of pins that are on the sites you will find. These are overseas Scrapper mills. Personally, when a pin is shown on these sites, we don't trade for it.

3.   Use your common sense. Trade for what is new in the park. Check the stores for starter sets and familiarize yourself with the current Hidden Mickey pins, so you have a decent chance of collecting legit pins.

4.   Don't freak out if you get a Scrapper or if someone tells you it's a Scrapper. My daughter had been hunting for a Tinkerbell pin that she finally found on a trip to WDW. She then had a veteran pin trader tell her the pin was a fake. She was devastated, and almost threw the pin away. After we calmed her down, we asked the well-meaning trader how we could identify a fake pin (we didn't know about Scrappers at the time) and she told us about the magnet test. She said that if you can't pick a pin up with a magnet, then it's a fake. Cool. Now we knew! On the way back to the hotel we picked up a magnet and started testing our pins. Based on "The Magnet Test" most of our pins were fake… including the ones we had just bought in the park. So much for a sure thing! The next day we had someone tell us that the way to detect a Scrapper using a magnet was that if you can pick it up… the bottom line… don't trust the magnet test! Scrappers are tough to spot except for the obvious tells described below, so if you see a pin you like, and it looks legit, trade for it. Unless you're going to resell it, the only person who going to worry about it is you… so why worry?   Okay, on with the CSI's…

CSI's—Common Scrapper Identifiers

Since Scrappers are now so common, we've actually begun to rate them based on the quality of the pin. The best quality of scrappers is the ones that are toughest to tell from the real pin and generally produced as an overrun from the authentic pin. Of course the preference should be to collect legitimate pins, but if you can't seem to find a pin you want you can keep the best scrapper you can find until a real one comes along...

The Real Pin:
Brighter Colors
Raised Metal Details
Smooth Edges
Thicker

Scrapper:
Faded Colors
Flat Metal Details
Rough Around & Edges
Thinner & Lighter

Here are some common identifiers to help you spot the fakes...

Quality of enamel — Authentic Disney pins have a glossy, bright finish. Like all things related to the Disney brand, presentation is everything! If you see a pin that looks dull and bland, there is a good chance that it's a scrapper. Other signs of concern in regards to the finish are bubbles in the enamel, discoloration, flaking or thin enamel and indents in the finish.

Color of Pin Detail — Compared to original pin, color will be a few shades off or faded from the usual bright colors associated with Disney pins. If Tigger is green instead of his usual bouncy orange, you might want to say TTFN on the trade...

Rough or Bumpy Edges — Rough or bumps where the pin was taken from the mold show the lack of care taken on scrappers. The longer the pin is copied, the worse the condition of the metal edge becomes. These pins are not polished or properly finished, and can even be molded from an inferior metal.

The Metal — On the worst of scrappers, the silver metal finish is plated or painted on and flakes off. You may also find areas filled in where the original pin has a gap because the pin has not been cleaned out or properly polished.

The Back Stamp — Variations on manufacturing or Disney stamp Icon, indentations are shallow or do not extend past the edge of the pin. As a general rule there should not be a border on the back of a pin, although we have gotten some pins recently directly from Disney with a border, so this isn't always 100%. Check with online resources, or ask the Facebook page crowd if you come across a pin with a border on the back and are unsure of its authenticity. In any case the back stamp should be very well defined. If the back stamp looks "blobby" it's a scrapper. Please keep in mind that there are numerous styles of back stamps on Disney pins. Finding a pin with a plain back does not mean it is a fake. Most vintage Disney pins came with a plain back and were not stamped with a design until around 2007, and even then it was inconsistent. Common back stamps are:

	Plain Gold or Silver	Vintage Disney pins, Hidden Mickey pins and early DSF pins (actually most early pins have a plain back)
	Grid or Hash Marks	Vintage Disney pins
	Mickey Head Icon	Disney Pins post 2007/2008
	Ice Cream Cone Icon	Disney Soda Fountain, Ghirardelli Soda Fountain, Disney Studio Store Hollywood
	Auction Gavel Icon	Disney Auctions
	Sorcerer Hat Icon	Walt Disney Imagineering (WDI)
	33	Disneyland's Club 33

Size of Pin — Scrappers are often a different size than the original or a totally different size or format; IE: the original pin was standard size and the scrapper version is a jumbo pin or vice versa.

Pin Variations & Detail — This may be in color, size or design details. In extreme cases the pin may be an entirely different color than the original. A common variation is a missing detail like a mouth or eye color. You will also find plain metal areas filled in where there is a gap or space on the original pin.

Timing and Location — When Disney releases a new series of Hidden Mickey pins, everyone gets excited and rushes to the park to start collecting them. In recent years, we were shocked to see that the WDW series was already available in Disneyland and vice versa! Then we double checked our enthusiasm and common sense, realizing that the pins were obviously scrappers. So, if a pin is available before its actual release or shows up in a different park on release day, you may want to question its authenticity. The good news is that the pin will probably a very good quality scrapper as it will be an "end of run" pin, which means it should be very difficult to see the difference from the original.

Here are some examples of Scrappers that we have found in the parks:

Got this one 2 months before it "officially" came out

Rough Bumps and Edges

We were excited to get this one until we saw the real one had a metal "40" on the face of it.

A blob backstamp, no defined "Mickey Head"

When is a Disney Pin, Not a Disney Pin?

We've already talked about Scrappers, and how bad they are for the Pin Trading Community. Let's talk about other pins that you may come across.

Officially Licensed Pins

Just like Disney has licensed their characters and artwork to companies for Commercials, T-shirts, and other merchandise, they have also licensed their artwork to a couple of companies to produce pins.

Jerry Leigh

Jerry Leigh is a clothing manufacturing company that specializes in resort & tourist items. These items range from apparel to branded household items, tote bags, purses, hats, and even collector pins. These Jerry Leigh pins, ARE official licensed Disney Pins, and they are sold in multiple retail outlets outside of the Disney Parks in both Orlando, FL and Anaheim, CA. Some of the places that you can find these pins are Target®, Wal-Mart®, Walgreens®, and many other chain locations.

These pins come on special backer cards that identify them as Officially Licensed Disney Pins. They are all different designs than what is sold within the parks, so make sure to check them out if you're in an area that has them. Unlike the pins in the parks, the actual designs that each store may have is completely random, so if you see a design you like buy it because you never know when you might see that one again.

ProPins

ProPins were created and sold in Germany in the late 1990's, these are authentic licensed Disney Pins. While much smaller than standard Disney Pins, they utilized a lot of different colors in their designs. Over the years that they were making pins, they created over 250 different designs, including some pretty amazing multi-pin sets that were and are sought after by collectors.

Sedesma

The Sedesma pins are sold all over Spain, they are sold in every type of store imaginable, including grocery stores. While these are authentic pins and are tradeable in the parks, they are usually of a lower quality manufacturing that normal Disney pins, so many collectors frown on them.

Hot Art, Ltd. / ACME Archives

One of the newest Official Licensees is Hot Art, Ltd. (Hot Art) which is based out of Hong Kong. In addition to selling their pins thru exclusive subscriptions in the United States and Europe, they also have an actual store in the Downtown Disney area of Disneyland Shanghai, China.

All of their designs are based off of actual licensed Disney artwork that has been produced and sold by ACME Archives for years. And now thru this special licensing agreement, Hot Art is making this artwork into very limited edition collectible pins. They have also gotten the licenses to make special Star Wars®

and Marvel® pins based on the ACME Artwork as well so you never know what they may be putting out in the future.

The first product developed by Hot Art was their Artist's Series Limited Edition 100 Jumbo Pins. Each of these amazing pins comes with a numbered lithograph of the original artwork that the design is based on all in a special designer box. These pins are only available via a monthly subscription direct from Hot Art, or via their website (online orders can only ship to addresses in Asia). The initial cost of these pins was $125.00 each, and they release approximately 4 per month.

For the opening of their store in Disneyland Shanghai, they also created a number of other series, including a Platinum Variation on the Artist's Series (the same or similar design but made out of silver metal instead of gold, and some differences in the enamel coloring), these Platinum Variants are also Limited Edition of 100, but are only available in person at the store in Shanghai and sell for approximately $250.00 each.

Then they created a series of higher edition pins, which are Limited Edition of 250. These LE250 pins come individually or as a set of 5, which includes an 11" x 17" Lithograph with spaces to put the 5 pins, and have it framed. Again, these are only available at the store in Shanghai or by special arrangement at a couple of pin trading events in the U.S. These pins retail at the Shanghai store for approximately $39.95 each. Some of these LE250 series have also had completer pins made to round out the set, but those have only been sold at special trading events around the world, so keep your eyes out for the notices of their release.

As of this edition of the book, there are also discussions of creating some super Jumbo Limited Edition of 50 pins, as well as some higher edition pins for the store in Shanghai, but there has been no discussion of having these other series available in other parts of the world.

If you are interested in collecting much higher end types of pins like these, please check out website at MousePinTrading.com where we have posted the flyers from Hot Art of all the pins they have released since they began distribution in October, 2015.

NOT Officially Licensed Pins

Scrappers, Again!

Now we've already talked about Scrappers a bunch of times, and how bad they are for the Pin Trading Community. To recap, Scrappers fall into 2 categories:

1) Over-runs and Quality Rejected Pins, these are the ones that were made from the same molds that are used for the Authentic Disney Pins, but have either failed Quality Control checks or in some cases were made from the original mold at the factory after hours, or even after the delivery of pins to Disney was complete. The tell-tale sign of these is that they are sold online (usually eBay)

direct from China or Hong Kong around the same time (or sometimes even before) or within a couple of months of the pin being released by Disney.

2) The 2nd type of Scrapper is one that is produced long after the fact. These are usually made by someone who gets the actual Disney pin and sends it to a factory to be copied. This is essentially a "counterfeit" pin, as it is not made from the same mold as the Authentic Disney Pin. These are usually slightly different from the original pin, either in colors, size, or some other factor that you can only tell by comparing the fake to the real one side-by-side.

Many new traders see pins be offered on eBay or Amazon for an extremely low price, usually around $1 per pin and jump at the chance to take some cheap pins to the park to trade and save money. Unfortunately when people do that, we all see the repercussions of that when we walk around the parks and 80% of the pins on cast member's lanyards are scrappers. These same traders get disappointed when they get all their newly traded for pins home and find out that a majority of them are scrappers themselves. The only way to combat this is to make sure that you are only getting real Disney pins. There are places to get Authentic Disney pins at prices much lower than you'll find in the parks and we cover many of them within the pages of this book.

'Fantasy' Pins

These aren't the pins of your dreams, but you may love some of the designs. Ever since there has been pin trading, there have been people (artists) who have come up with their own doodles, designs, and ideas for making pins, just like Disney does. Before we get into more about Fantasy Pins, we want to be 100% clear with you, **Fantasy Pins are ILLEGAL**, they violate both Copyright Law by using Disney's Characters or their likenesses without permission, and Trademark Law, as all the different characters are also trademarked by Disney.

Some people argue that Fantasy Pins, or Fan-Art is covered under the Fair Use Clause in the Copyright Law, we are not lawyers and wouldn't want to mislead anyone into thinking that these pins are ok, so we will restate that from everything that we have seen and been told, the creators of Fantasy Pins are breaking the law. It is up to you as a collector as to whether you would want to add these types of pins to your collection or not, that is entirely your decision.

There are a few different types of Fantasy Pins out there, some can be found for sale on eBay and others can be traded for with other Pin Traders, but under no circumstances are Fantasy Pins tradeable in the parks or with Cast Members.

Here are some common types of Fantasy Pins:

- They sometimes contain character combinations that don't fit the "Disney" theme. Usually called "mash-ups" these are cross overs of characters from different un-related movies or shows that wouldn't normally be seen. i.e.: Rapunzel & Flynn in the boat scene from The Little Mermaid, or Snow White dancing with Gaston, etc.
- They are usually much smaller edition sizes than anything that Disney normally makes; we have seen them as small as Limited Edition of 15.
- Many of the Fantasy pins are either much larger or much smaller than standard Disney Pins. We have seen Fantasy pins up to 5" tall and as small as ¾" tall. Do not mistake all small pins for Fantasy, as the Sedesma & ProPins that are created in Europe are frequently "mini pins" but aren't fantasy pins.
- Of course, there are also some very inappropriate (adult themed) and not Disney-like pins that are created as well, although these are more rare and harder to find.
- On many of them without seeing the back of the pin to look for the ©Disney backstamp, there is no way to tell, so please check carefully any pin that you get to make sure you know what you have. Most reputable traders and sellers will clearly identify it as a "Fantasy Pin", but there are always exceptions.

Even though we have provided images for most of the sections of this book to help illustrate the various types of pins, back stamps, themes, etc. we will not be showing any examples of Fantasy Pins in this book as we respect Disney's ownership of their copyright and trademarks over the various Disney characters.

Now, on with the book...

Pin Trading Essentials

Tools of the Trade:

To get started in trading Disney Pins, you need a few essential tools:

1. Something to put your pins on (or in)
2. A few extra pin backs
3. A big smile
4. A great attitude
5. Pins (obviously!)
6. This Book! *Seriously... take me with you!*

Okay, so having pins is a no-brainer, but where can you buy them before you get to Disney? There are actually quite a few options open to you, but first, let's look at what else you need.

Something to put your pins on...

We've never seen anyone refuse to trade a pin with someone who kept their pins in a plastic bag, but there are better ways to manage your pin inventory! The most popular is an adult or child sized lanyard which hangs around your neck and holds your pins through the nylon mesh. These can be purchased through Disneystore.com or on EBay before you leave, and this is a great way to get your family into the excitement of trading. You can either choose or have them choose a lanyard with their favorite Disney character or theme.

We've seen people make their own lanyards out of strips of nylon ribbon and Velcro, but unless budget is a serious, concern, we recommend you invest the $8.95 in a proper Disney Pin Lanyard, to get you in the spirit. If you wait until you're in the park, make lanyard shopping one of the first things on your list!

You can also purchase Pin Starter Sets in a variety of character themes that include the lanyard. These sets usually retail around $24.95 and $44.95 depending on how many pins are included. The risk with these sets is that they came with really cool pins of your favorite character, so some folks (especially the younger ones!) have a hard time trading these pins away, or even trading back for them, so if you are going this route, try to find the sets that come with two of each pin, which gives you one to trade and one to keep.

This set has 8 funky Mickey Pins that you may want to keep...

This Starter Set has:

One set of pins to keep ->

And One set of pins to trade ->

Once you've picked out your lanyard, you can personalize it even more with a Lanyard Medallion, which also helps keep your lanyard from bouncing around as you're running to get a picture with Tigger! Some of these medallions are Open Edition and some are a Limited Release or available only at Pin Trading events. Find one you like and attach it to the loop at the bottom of your lanyard.

If the thought of something hanging around your neck all day doesn't appeal to you, you might want to consider a Hip Lanyard or Pin Bag. The Hip Lanyard is a patch of nylon that hangs from your belt and the Disney Pin Bag is just what it sounds like... a shoulder bag that holds and displays your pins. They retail between $20.00 and $50.00, although you can sometimes get lucky on an EBay auction.

Pin bags are great when you are setting up shop in the park (at specified locations only) but they can get heavy and bulky when you are moving through the park and on and off the attractions. There are smaller versions available that work well and you can always put your trading pins on the strap itself if you like. Here are a few pics of one of our bags...

Mouse Pin Trading Tip!

All Disney Pin Trading bags have 2 or 3 zippered pouches for holding extra pins, pin backs, pin lists, and whatever else you can stuff in there plus velveteen pouches to display your pins. We were given a great tip from another Pin Trader (Thanks to Ron from Anaheim, CA!) to put cardboard or foam board into the display pouches so that you don't have to deal with the pin backs when trading on a tabletop.

The board holds the pins securely and saves time (and pricked fingers) when moving the pins. Keep an eye out if you use cardboard though, because the pins will eventually work their way loose. My personal preference is a double sheet of foam board or better yet "Gator Board". But be careful with "Gator Board" as it is harder and you may bend the posts on the pins if you aren't careful with it.

Managing Your Pins

Once you get rolling and start running from Cast Member to Cast Member trading pins at every opportunity, you might find yourself forgetting what you have and what you don't have and when it comes to Hidden Mickey Pins, what you're collecting and what you aren't!

We have run into the unfortunate situation where we mistakenly trade away pins that we meant to keep, and nothing is worse than asking "Where's that pin that I've been looking for 6 months that I got today" and then vaguely remember trading it away because it was mixed in with your traders. It happened to us, so now we have a system... two systems actually.

Pin System 1: Keepers and Traders

Pick a side of your lanyard for keepers and another for traders. My daughter uses this system for her pins and she makes sure she knows which is which by putting an anchor pin on each side; Tinkerbell for keepers and a Puffle (those fuzzy things from Club Penguin) for Traders. Why Tink and a Puffle? Because Tink is her favorite and she doesn't have the same appreciation for the Puffles! That way, even in the frenzy of pin trading with multiple cast members, when she looks down at her lanyard, she knows exactly where to take the trader from and where to put the new find!

It is simple but effective. But what happens when the Keeper Side gets full? Enter...

Pin System 2: The Bag Man

That would be me. Or maybe in your case, someone else in your group with the ability to be left holding the bag... of pins. I carry a smaller Pin Bag with two zipper pouches that hold only keepers for the entire group. This leaves the rest of the group to keep only traders on their lanyards. When they trade for a pin they want to keep, they give it to me and I put it in the back pouch.

If there is a pin they have traded up for (IE: Rack Pin for a Limited Edition or Completer Pin), but it's on the bubble, then I put it into the front pouch. Both pouches get emptied out at the end of the day, so we can decide as a group which pins to keep and which pins become more valuable traders.

Then we make note of what we still need to complete the series (the checklists in this book are good for that) and restock the lanyards for the next day!

To keep your newly found pins secure, you might want to consider picking up a few extra Rubber Mickey Pin Backs, which secure your pins to your lanyard. Each pin you trade comes with an authorized pin back, but you will lose a back here and there, so it's a good idea to have back up. A package of Pin Backs can be purchased at most retail locations in the park, but if you happen to lose one, simply ask a Cast Member or fellow pin trader if they have any extras.

Disney sells Locking Pin Backs which are great if you have special pins that you want to display on your lanyard or pin bag. They come with a small allen wrench to lock your pin in place and are very secure. Beware of this type of locking pin back, if you accidentally tighten it too much, you can risk bending or breaking the pin post. Also, the locking pin backs from Disney use a strange sized allen wrench, so if you lose it, you will not be able to easily get it open.

There is another type of locking pin back which is more like those used on men's tie tacks, which have a twist lock piece on the back. These are a little more expensive, but are much safer for your pins. You can find this type on Amazon or eBay for a good price.

That covers all you need for the physical elements of Pin Trading, but we're not joking about the big smile and good attitude. When trading in the park, it can get pretty interesting when you meet someone who pushes through the line to get a pin they see on a Cast Member's lanyard. Pin Trading should be an enjoyable experience for everyone and when guests get impatient or rude, it brings everyone down.

Pin Trading Etiquette

We are going to copy the Pin Trading Etiquette Rules directly from the Disney Pin Trading site so that you have it for reference, but we would like to add a couple of points.

Point 1: When you see a Cast Member who is on task, be patient and polite. If they are doing something critical like serving another guest or setting up parade routes, please be respectful of their time. Make eye contact, let them know you are there and when they are done with their task, they will trade with you. We have even had Cast Members track us down to complete a trade after we thought they had ducked out.

If the Cast Member who you want to trade with is working a busy cash register in one of the retail locations, consider getting in line with the guests waiting to purchase their items. Once they know you want to trade, many Cast Members will take off their lanyards and let you browse while they look after other guests. It's a good idea to get a look at their pins from afar (without being creepy!) to see if there is anything you want a closer look at.

Hip lanyards have a tendency to flip over (or the Cast Member has turned it over on purpose) so use your discretion when asking to see their pins. We've never been refused, but there have been times when we definitely got the feeling we were interrupting... in pleasant way of course.

Point 2: No matter who you are trading with, be respectful of them and their pins. This should go without saying, but some guests can get pretty enthusiastic when it comes to trading and they may not be familiar with the etiquette.

When we started trading, it took a while to get the rhythm and even longer for the kids to understand that they didn't have to trade with everyone they see. As you become more comfortable with pin trading, share your experience and knowledge with newer traders. (known as Newbies)

The idea behind pin trading is to meet people, so ask other Disney guests in line for attractions to see their pins. Worst case scenario is that you pass the time waiting to get on the attraction (especially good advice on Toy Story Mania!). We also carry a few extra pins around for **"Random Acts of Pinning"** where the kids give out pins to younger guests (with their parent's permission) who might not be as patient as we "more seasoned" Disney guests. It's  amazing to see the reaction of the people around you and occasionally a nearby Cast Member has rewarded the kids for their generosity. We even hand out a few pins on the plane on the way down.

Okay, now that that's done, here's the Etiquette section from the Disney pin Trading Site:

Disney Pin Trading Etiquette

> Have Fun! Disney Pin Trading can be a great way to interact with and meet Cast Members and other guests

> The main criteria to judge whether a pin is tradable or not is that it must be a metal pin that represents a Disney Event, Location, Character, or Icon. Some pins from our Operating Participants are also tradable,, but must represent the Operating Participant in a way that has a specific Disneyland Resort or Walt Disney World Resort Affiliation.

> Pins should be in good, undamaged condition.

> Trade one pin at a time, hand to hand, with the backs attached

> Guests may trade a maximum of two pins with each Cast Member

> Guests may trade only one pin of the same style with a Cast Member.

> When trading with Cast Members, Guests should offer a pin that is not already displayed on the Cast Member's lanyard.

> Please refrain from touching another person's pins or lanyard. If you need a closer look, ask the person wearing the lanyard if they can bring it into clearer view for you.

> Disney name pins may not be traded with Cast Members

> Monies or gifts may not be exchanged or used in trade for a pin.

> In addition to the 12 pins on the Cast Lanyards, some Cast Members may wear a "Showcase" pin. These "Showcase" pins are for demonstrations to our guests and are not available for trade.

Now you've got everything you need... oh wait. What about pins?

Where to get your Trading Pins...

There are lots of places to get pins and some are more cost effective than others! You can wait until you are on your Disney vacation to get your pins, but there are more cost effective options that may be less expensive and less stressful (see Chapter 2) based on our family's experience. There is no reason for you to break the bank and you can have a good selection of trading pins before you leave for your Disney Dream vacation. Just be aware that when you buy lower priced pins on line you may be opening yourself up to fake pins or scrappers.

If you are going to wait until you arrive in the park to purchase your pins, make sure you purchase a few starter sets (the 7 pin or lanyard sets are a slightly better deal on a "cost per pin basis" and retail between $29.95 and $49.95) to get you rolling. Most retail locations in Disney Parks have a selection of pins and starter packs, but there are a few key locations in each park. You can find a listing of recommended retail locations in the resource section at the back of the book, or for the most up to date information, check MousePinTrading.com.

NOTE! The best way to ensure that you are buying Authentic Disney Pins is to purchase them from Disney in a Disney Park or an online Disney retailer. It will cost you a little more, but at least you know that you are trading authentic pins. If you are going to purchase your trading pins online, ask around for a reputable source. Look for personal collections and auctions that show you the actual pins you will be bidding on.

Here are a few other options for you:

Buying Pins On eBay or Amazon

If you are able to plan ahead, you can order your pins on line for a very reasonable cost per pin. Look for pin collections that say they are tradable in the Disney Parks and do not contain Scrappers, Propins or Sedesmas. But here's the deal... when you're paying $1 or less per pin, there is a very good chance you're buying scrappers. You can tell yourself they said "Authentic Disney Pins" and "100% Tradable" but to be honest... If you want to limit your exposure to buying scrappers, bid on pin lots that show you the actual pins you are going to get. Random pin lots = scrappers... we just wanted to be clear on that.

That said... At least a month before you go (at this point, we always have an inventory of traders on hand) search EBay for "Disney Pin Collection". You will find pin lots of 10, 20, 25, and 50 and up to 200 and 300 that you can bid on and win at less than $1.00 per pin. Since scrappers have flooded the market, we try to avoid RANDOM PIN LOTS, as we have to assume that the lot will contain some Scrappers. Even when the auction states that the pins have been traded in Disney Parks, it does not guarantee that the pins are Authentic Disney Pins, as there are a ton of Scrappers sitting on Cast Member lanyards.

It's your call, but fake pins dilute the value and more importantly, the enjoyment of collecting Disney Pins. If it seems too good to be true, it probably is... We still buy bulk lots of pins from trusted Ebayers, but when we get an obvious Scrapper Pin, we do as the name says and scrap it. Okay, back to how to buy your trading pins on Ebay...

The reason we advise you shop at least 30 days prior to your trip is that you need the auction to end and allow enough time for shipping. Some sellers will ship to your Disney resort, but we prefer to have them in our hot little hands before we leave!

Although you can find some decent "Buy It Now" pricing, you generally get a better deal through the auction. Remember, these pins are for trading, so you don't really care what pins are in the collection and buying collections will save you on shipping fees versus buying individual pins.

When purchasing pins online, there are a couple of points that I have found useful. If you are not familiar with purchasing on

EBay, take some time to browse around and familiarize yourself with where the pertinent information is located.

Who Do You Buy from?

Personally, we don't buy from anyone with less than a 98% EBay score (preferably 100%) with a decent number of completed transactions (look for the EBay Preferred Seller Status) and decent feedback. Unfortunately a high Seller Rating doesn't ensure that the pins you are buying are Authentic Disney Pins, so check the comments and more importantly where the pins are shipping from and what they look like.

To avoid buying scrappers, we try to buy what looks like a collection instead of a "pin lot". You can pick up a decent selection of pins (sometimes with the bag) for $1.00 or $2.00 per pin, and you have a better chance of getting authentic Disney Pins. When you find a seller you like, save them to your Favorite Seller List so you can get notified when they have more pins for sale. The bottom line is that $2 is still better than $9 per pin when you're on a budget.

Choose a seller who agrees to ship within 1-3 days, with a tracking number if possible and estimate at least 5-10 days for transit and delivery. We found a great resource (Thanks Kevin H!) where you can check the feedback and comments on any eBay Seller. For this resource, the comments are the most important part, as you can look for words like, Scrapper and Fake to identify sellers that deal in aftermarket pins. We're not responsible or affiliated with it, so you're on your own here, but here's the site if you're curious:

http://www.toolhaus.org/cgi-bin/negs

Again, when you find someone you like, save them into your favorite sellers so you can go back to them for your next trip. If they ship to the Park resorts and you happen to run out of pins, they can be a handy resource who can hook you up with pins on short notice. (It happens!) Sellers from Florida and Southern California are obviously near the parks, so have access to newer pins, but we have great success with sellers from across the US and Canada who are dumping their "post vacation" collections!

Since writing the first edition of this book, we have built up a huge collection of pins for sale and have started our own eBay store (MousePinTrader.com), and also a dedicated online store (MousePinTradingPost.com). On both of these stores we have a wide assortment of pins, everything from Hidden Mickey Pins, all the way to ultra-rare Framed Pin Sets. See the section on the next page under "Trusted Online Sellers" for a special coupon code to our online store.

Trusted Secondary Resellers in the Los Angeles Area:

Frank and Son Collectible Show

19649 San Jose Ave., City of Industry, CA 91748 (frankandsonshow.net)

This place is awesome! You might want to plan to spend a few hours (or the whole day!) wandering the aisles of Frank & Son's if you decide to venture out in search of Disneyana! This indoor flea market / collectible warehouse features hundreds of exhibitors who sell everything under the SoCal sun… including Disney Pins! At last check, there were 4 booths that dealt in Disney Pins, but that can change monthly. Check their website for their days and hours, as of our last visit, they were only open on Wednesday from 3pm-9pm and Saturday from 9am-3pm.

Here you may find that elusive pin to complete your Hidden Mickey collection or grab bags of trading pins. It's worth the trip. If you go, make sure you stop by booth #518 and say Hello to Melinda. She is a wealth of knowledge, very fair, and great to trade with and buy from. We make a point of going there every time we're in California. Their Facebook page: https://www.facebook.com/frankandsonshow/

My-D Pins & Collectibles

1215 S. Beach Blvd., Suite D, Anaheim, CA 92804 (mydpins.com)

A little closer to home and highly recommended by our friend and fellow pin trader, Disneyland Dan, this shop has a ton of funky and hard to find Disney Pins and Disneyana. Josue (Josh) sells all kinds of collectibles but specializes in Disney. He has a wealth of knowledge and given enough time, will be able to track down that elusive Disney pin you've been looking for! His prices are very reasonable and deals only in authentic Disney Pins. You can also buy from his eBay store. His Facebook Page is:

https://www.facebook.com/mydpins. On our last trip to California, one of us found a Limited Edition of 100 Captain Hook pin that we have been looking for, for years.

Trusted Secondary Resellers in the Orlando Area:

Booster Packs and Beyond

8548 W. Irlo Bronson Memorial Hwy (Hwy 192), Kissimmee, FL

Our friend Michelle runs this shop out of the Gate West Flea Market. They have a good selection of pins for sale at very good prices, including booster packs, pins on cards. Their Facebook page is: https://www.facebook.com/boosterpacksandbeyond/

Character Corner

5283 W. Irlo Bronson Memorial Hwy (Hwy 192), Kissimmee, FL

This shop is one of the better shops selling all things Disney and Universal from t-shirts, and gifts to pins and other old collectibles. Ask Akram to see the more exclusive pins that he keeps just for real collectors and traders. You can find their Facebook page here: https://www.facebook.com/CharacterCornerFL/

Trusted Online Sellers:

MousePinTradingPost.com

The authors of this book have an online store where we sell some of the pins that we have purchased over the years. To thank you for purchasing our book, we would like to give you 10% off any items purchased from us. Just use Coupon Code: "2016Book" when placing your order to get your 10% Discount.

Do You Buy From China or Europe?

It's up to you, but our preference is to shop within the US and Canada. In our experience, we have received a higher number of "Scrapper" pins from China and it's a bit suspicious when they send pins that aren't even in circulation yet! Of course all Disney pins are made in China (it says so right on the back!) which is why you will find a high number of scrappers coming from overseas. We already talked about "Scrappers", and how to spot them, but with great pin trading comes great responsibility (Disney owns Marvel Comics, so it's okay to quote Uncle Ben from

Spiderman) and it's a good thing to keep fake pins out of circulation as they devalue the real pins.

If you do choose to buy from Overseas, take note that it can take up to 45 days to receive your pins, so plan accordingly. Also make sure you know what the shipping costs are going to be before you bid.

What Pins Do You Buy?

Whatever fits within your budget! If you are intending on trading mainly with Cast Members then it doesn't matter how cool and funky your pins are. You are buying them to be traded, so you don't want to get emotionally attached to your pin inventory!

When buying on line, we try to bid on the biggest personal collections I can find within our budget, so we don't end up paying a lot of extra shipping charges. Generally, the larger the lot, the better your price per pin is going to be. If bidding on multiple lots from the same seller, we make sure to ask for combined shipping so we don't get double charged.

Duplicates (in pin lot of 100 or more) are okay, especially if you are just starting out, as you will have some pins that you want to keep for your collection. Just like the pin lanyard sets, you now have one to keep and one to trade. When a retailer says they  "Carry 50 different styles at a time" they are probably buying Scrappers directly from overseas manufacturers. Like we said before... Scrappers are evil.

Shipping

Make sure you know what the shipping costs are before you bid and compare a few different sellers. As the pin market has become more competitive, many sellers are offering free shipping as an incentive. Always keep your "landed" or total cost in mind. Set a target price per pin including shipping, so you can stay on budget. Your goal should be to get as many pins as you can for your budget.

It's a good idea to know the approximate shipping costs so you don't get taken advantage of by sellers who are padding the margin on shipping. A USPS Small Flat

Rate Priority Mail Box can hold 100 pins and costs $5.95 (as of the time of this publication). Some sellers will add in a couple of bucks for their time, packaging and gas and I am fine with that as long as they tell you in the description and it's within budget.

A SPECIAL NOTE FOR CANADIANS, Eh? Shipping to Canada from the US can be expensive, slow and limit the amount of sellers you can buy from. If you live within driving distance of the US border, there are numerous shipping houses that you can ship to for a small fee (Our guy charges $2.50 per shipment) to avoid the issues. Some sellers don't like to ship to anything other than your PayPal address, so make sure they will ship to a third party address. If they won't ship, find a new seller; there are dozens of quality sellers who want your business.

PayPal

If you are new to EBay, you will need to set up a PayPal Account to pay for your transaction. Its EBay's preferred currency and you attach your account to a credit card or bank account. It takes minutes to set up and actually gives you insurance should you happen to have a dispute with the seller.

Remember why you're buying the pins – worth saying again!

FOR TRADING! You don't care if you have duplicates or how many Tinkerbell pins are in the lot, you're going to trade them away! There are always going to be a few keepers in any pin lot you buy, so bump your numbers by 10 or 20% to account for the AAAWWWWW LOOOOOKKKK AAAATTT THIIIIISSSSSS OOONNNEEEE!!!!! Factor.

It happens every time we get an order in... even with 3000+ pins in the collection!

Disney Outlet or Disney Character Outlet Stores.

We recommend to people who are visiting a Disney Park for the first time to stop by one of these stores before going to the park if they have time. These two chains are

the authorized clearance locations for Disney Parks and you can find some huge discounts (up to 80% off) on all kinds of Disney merchandise including pins! The average price for pins here is between $4 and $7 but you can sometimes find even lower prices on pins they can't clear out or that are dated (IE: Bosses Day 2004!). We have found great pins for trading here, and we have also found just plain great pins. On our first trip to the Disney Character Outlet Store in Fullerton, CA, we found almost all of the Gold 50th Anniversary Character pins for $5 each that were tough to find on the secondary market.

You never know what you may find!

These stores come and go, but there is usually one or two around Orlando, FL and Anaheim, CA and they often put temporary locations in outlet malls throughout the US. We have personally found temporary Disney Outlet Stores (or partial Disney Outlet Stores) in Seattle, WA, Las Vegas, NV and Honolulu, HI, and actually completed Limited Edition Series from their sale inventory. It's a great way to find higher value pins below market value.

The Disneystore.com

Disney used to run an online outlet store, but has since consolidated their online retail into one site. Click on the bottom of the page for SALE items which, of course, includes a decent selection of pins.

These pins are not usually better priced than in the Parks (in fact many of them are the same as they offer Park Merchandise, which can be handy if you get home and realize that you just can't do without that pin you saw in the Emporium or need to buy just one more Mystery Set), but they do go on sale from as low as $4.95 and, if you time it right, the seasonal boxed sets can be a great deal.

Make sure you pay attention to the shipping costs, as they can be expensive on smaller orders, and often run free shipping promotions with a minimum order.

Other Opportunities

If you live in California or Florida you will often find Disney Pins for sale on Craig's List and other online community services, but the majority of these listings are Collectors who are looking to sell higher value collections.

For the local Disneyana Fan who doesn't mind getting up early and hitting the streets, you can find some pretty cool pins at garage sales and flea markets. We've met some Pin Traders in Disneyland who have found entire Vintage pin collections in garage sale give away boxes, but you better get there early and not rely too heavily on filling your trader quota the Saturday morning before you get to the park!

Personally, seeing as we don't live close to a Disney Park (my wife doesn't consider 23 hours of straight driving close), we keep track of which of our friends have been to Disney recently and when we see them, we ask "Did you collect any pins when you were there?" We know it's not rocket science, but it's amazing how many of them have pins they don't want and will offer to give them away! By the way, we generally trade a few smaller pins for a cool duplicate pin that I have on hand, so that we're not taking advantage of them.

When we are in the park, we will also keep an eye out for pins that our friends collect and bring them back for them so they will return the favour when they go back.

Who do you know with a drawer full of Vintage pins they don't want? You could even try posting a "Disney Pins Wanted" ad in your local paper or on Craig's List.

In Disney Parks

Okay, so you bought the book, but didn't get around to buying your pins in advance. No worries, you can get your pins in the park. You will pay a bit more, but you can get your pins in the park.

Here's the deal. Get the most you can for your dollar.

When you're looking at pin sets, do the math on what it costs per pin versus the retail cost of the set. Last time I checked the best deal was the 7 pin set for $29.95 or $4.27 per pin.

When you are buying pins, we recommend purchasing in an actual Pin Store instead of the other 50 or so shops that have a pin display. The reason for this is that the pin stores will have the Gift with Purchase Collections and the other stores may not.

Check out what the amount is (usually around $30) and ask the Cast Member if you can get more than one Mystery (GWP) pin with a larger purchase or if you need to break it up into smaller purchases. Then work out the values so you can get the most Disney bang for your buck.

It's always better to group your purchases, but if you can't resist the urge to pop into the first store you see and buy pins, make sure you save your receipts. If you ask nicely, the Cast Member in the Pin Shop will usually let you add them up and then mark the receipt.

In Disneyland, CA try the Westward Ho Trading Company in Frontierland and Little Green Men in Tomorrowland.

In Walt Disney World there are a few more options, but our favorites are The Frontier Trading Company in Frontierland and Mouse Gears in Epcot.

Okay, so let's run a quick inventory:

Alright, give everyone a High Five, take a deep breath, and let's go trade some pins!

Everyone's pin backs on tight? We are going to go through this point by point with the...

✓ Lanyard
✓ Pin Bag
✓ Extra Pin Backs
✓ At Least 25 Pins per Person
✓ Attitude (or Lack Thereof)
✓ This Book (of course)

The A-Z of Mouse Pin Trading Tips for an Awesome Pin Trading Experience!

 **Allow time to trade.** Nothing is more frustrating than having part of your group rushing to get on an attraction or meet a character and have someone stop every 20 feet to trade pins, and vice versa. The way we handle this is to have one of us take the tickets and go Fast Pass an attraction or get line for a character and meet back up with the pin traders. It really helps manage the time. NOTE: The person who goes on the errand should have pins with them just in case they see something worth trading for on the way!

 **Be polite.** Although Disney Cast Members are always open to trading (see Tip E), they still have a job to do in the park. If you see someone who you want to trade with, but they are in the middle of something or with another guest, be patient. Once they see you, they will generally acknowledge you and trade with you once they are done. If you are in a store and the Cast Member is at a busy cash register, you may want to get in line and wait with the people purchasing. If you ask to see a Cast Members pins and they have nothing you want to trade for, you are not obligated to trade, but again, be polite and thank them for their time. A little courtesy will go a long way with Disney.

 **Child Only Lanyards.** Green (WDW) or Teal (DL) Lanyards and Hip Pouches are for trading with guests between the age of 3 and 12. This gives the kids a fair chance of finding cool pins without competing with the big guys. If you have someone in your party who is in that age range, encourage them to trade, as the Cast Members with the Child Lanyards are trained to be especially nice to the younger traders and will encourage them to keep trading. This means that as a parent you need to back off and let the magic happen. Recently the child only lanyards practice seems to be less and less available and is up to the individual cast member.

Do not leave any traders at home. Bring the whole lot with you. Why? Because remember those pins that everyone fell in love with when you opened the package at your kitchen table? Well, you are about to enter a world where that experience is going to repeat itself every 20 feet or so... and we Pin Traders are fickle creatures! What was an untradeable pin before you left home can suddenly become fair game when you see a Cast Member with a cool pin of your favorite character or the one pin you need to complete a pin series. You can always take it back home with you, and when you are putting 20 or so pounds of pins in your carry-on, an extra pin or 2 isn't going to make a difference!

Every Cast Member wearing a black lanyard will trade with you. The only stipulations are that you can only trade up to a maximum of two pins per person and that the pin you are trading is not already on their lanyard. As long as they are wearing a Disney Cast Member Tag and a pin lanyard, you are good to go! A lot of Cast Members have moved to a Hip Pouch for trading, so you need to keep an eye out as they are harder to spot than regular lanyards. When seeking out black lanyards to trade with, it's a good idea to also make sure that the person you spotted is also wearing a Cast Member Name Tag... Our kids are famous for accosting unsuspecting guests who happen to be wearing a black lanyard! On the upside, they've never been refused a trade... but they are pretty persuasive!

Flying To Disney? Put your pins in your carry on as they can add pounds to your luggage. It's also kind of funny (as long as you have time) when the TSA agent asks you to show them your pins... slowly... so that they can have a look. Also if your pin bag is on the plane with you, you can kill some time going through your pins and checklists while you are in the air and maybe even trade a few pins on the plane. We usually end up giving away a few pins on the plane to families who are visiting Disney for the first time. Little do they know that the pin we gave them probably started them on a life of obsessive pin trading! Maybe next time, we should give them a copy of the book instead... and a pin.

Guest Relations In all Walt Disney World Parks have a Pin Trading Bag! Guests who happen to stop into the Guest Relations Building in Walt Disney World and patiently wait to ask if you can see the pin bag will be rewarded by a fantastic selection of pins that are continually "beefed" up by the Guest Relations Cast Members. The same rules apply as with trading from a Cast Lanyard: You can trade up to 2 pins per person and the pins you are trading shouldn't be in the pin book, but the rules seem to be a little more relaxed when trading from the bag...

Hidden Amongst Those Really Cool Buildings are secret passages that Cast Members travel in and out of as they go on and off shift. If you are careful not to act like a stalker or be a pain to someone who is trying to get home or onto the next scheduled task (Characters use some of these same secret doorways) it can be a great place to catch Cast Members who are loaded down with new pins on their lanyards as they come ON shift. Notice the big "ON"? When they are leaving the public areas of the park, they're trading day is done, so chances are their lanyards are full of the boring pins you've been seeing all day. When they are coming ON shift, that's when the good stuff comes out! Of course, occasionally they will just swap lanyards, so don't be disappointed! In Disneyland California, pay attention to the alley where the lockers are on Main Street, just behind the fruit stand. There's a great Ice Cream Shop down there too!

If you are doing anything Disney Related - Take your pins with you! This includes trips to the Disney Studio Store Hollywood in California, Downtown Disney (Disney Springs), or the Disney Character Outlets in Orlando. It should also include a trip to any major shopping center around a Disney park that might have a Disney Vacation Club Kiosk! – Yep, they have Pins! You never know who will be trading pins. We got burned once at the Disney Soda Fountain Shop in Hollywood and it will never happen again. It was our last evening in LA and the Cast Member working the fountain had 3 pins we needed to complete our series. The good news was that the Soda Fountain has a store attached to it that sells discount pins so we only spent $15.00 on additional pins to trade when we had a hundred or so traders sitting back in our hotel room! **Lesson learned – BRING YOUR PINS!**

Just when you thought you were done a Series... that's when you notice that there are little silver pins that look just like the ones you have or another pin that looks like it belongs to the series you just finished! Yep, there's a Chaser or a Completer pin for the series that wasn't in the guide, on the checklist or even on the Disney site. We do the best we can and most times we will let you know even before Disney does when a Completer Pin is spotted, but it won't make it into the book right away. The best way to make sure you don't leave the park blissfully (until you see the Completer online) unaware that you still need ONE MORE PIN! Is to ask a Cast Member. They might even have one saved for you... if you ask nicely and maybe cry a little...

Keep an eye out for Managerial and Custodial Staff. Unlike the folks in the stores, these Cast Members move around more and may have a better selection of Hidden Mickey pins. Anyone wearing a suit in a Disney Park is doing a walk-through from one of the divisions and is usually loaded with pins! This is especially true early in the morning and at the start of the afternoon and evening shifts. The Cast Member pin selection tends to get less exciting as the evening wears on, but the evening shift Cast Members may have just the pin you're looking for. We've found some great pins after dark and the stroller traffic is tucked away for the night. A Mickey light-up souvenir can come in handy here!

Limited Release and Surprise Pins can pop up anywhere and anytime so keep an eye out for them when you are browsing the pin shops. The Disney Studio Store Hollywood in California is famous for Surprise Pin Releases and they go quick as they are usually an LE of 150! Luck and timing need to be on your side and you need to be in the right place at the right time, but as with any other pin trading adventure, it never hurts to ask what's coming out. Check the blogs, the message boards and of course our Facebook group for announcements. Also be on the lookout for crowds of Pin Traders who happen to be lurking near a store... a surprise may be afoot!

 **Main Street USA in Walt Disney World is home to Scoop!** If you've been to Walt Disney World before, you've probably seen or heard of the Characters who reside there. I'm not talking about Mickey & Minnie, but instead the Mayor, Smokey the Fire Chief, and my very good friend Scoop Sanderson, who is the local newspaper reporter. Since the beginning of Pin Trading, Scoop has been the ultimate Pin Trading Expert at Walt Disney World, giving Pin Talks to teach guests about Disney Pins, and trading some of the most amazing pins I've ever gotten. But recently, his responsibilities at the newspaper have taken up most of his time. ☹ However, if you're on Main Street at Walt Disney World and you run into Scoop, make sure you introduce yourself to him and tell him that Mark & Ron from the Mouse Pin Guide told you to stop by and say "Hi!", you never know he may have a pin tucked away somewhere to trade with you.

 **New Pin Releases – It's all in the Wristband!** When Disney releases a very limited edition pin series or is releasing pins that are associated with a special Disney event, like the recent 30th Anniversary of EPCOT in Walt Disney World, or the Diamond (60th) Anniversary at Disneyland, they implement a wristband procedure for the release. First dibs on the product will go to those guests with a wristband, and entry into the retail locations will be staggered depending on the color of your wristband. These special releases usually include a variety of products, including pins, Vinylmation figures and other collectibles, so not everyone in line is a Pin Trader. These events can be a lot of fun, but be prepared to wait in line for several hours, beginning very early in the morning!

 **Other Trading Opportunities.** Each Disney Park has unique trading opportunities that are sometimes easy to spot, and sometimes more elusive. For example; Each Park in WDW has a pin book that is available to trade from. All you have to do is ask to see it at Guest Services or City Hall. Also, several stores and hotels will have

a Pin Board (or shield, or post, or hat or Donald Duck and yes even a Pin Stroller!) that you can trade from. Sometimes they are out in the open but quite often you will need to ask to see them. We had a list of them in the last version of the book, and we realized very quickly that these locations change too frequently to put a list in print, so you will just need to check around while you're walking thru the parks.

At certain times in Disneyland, just outside of the Westward Ho Trading Company Store in Frontierland, Cast Members will bring out pins bags for trading. This is a great opportunity to trade with a larger selection of pins and start trading with other guests who are in line to trade with the Cast Members. We've made some great trades and met some great people in these lines and quite often someone will track down a pin for you. You can check with Cast Members in the Westward Ho! for trading times or just look in the daily park guide.

Professional Pin Traders are also in the parks (Disneyland and Epcot) and will have books of pins available for trade. We have met some who are phenomenal to deal with and some who, unfortunately seem to be there to take advantage of novice traders, so beware.

Pin Trading Nights and Events have been held on an on-going basis at all the Disney Parks Worldwide, but in the last year or two, both Walt Disney World® in Florida and Disneyland® in California have drastically cut back or even stopped holding these events all together. Fortunately there have been a couple of local Pin Trading Groups, like ours who have stepped up and started holding monthly or quarterly pin trading events near the various parks. Since this is an on-going thing, you can check the Events Section of our website at: MousePinTrading.com/event-calendar/ for the latest information on events around the world. If you are new to pin trading come prepared with some questions that you would like to have answered. Most veteran pin traders don't mind spending time with Newbies so make sure you start of by telling them that you are new to Disney Pin Trading.

Quick Trading Opportunities are everywhere in Disney Parks if you know what to look for! This is probably one of my favorite tips because it usually equals a whole lot of fun in the park and it can get you a whole bunch of pins in just a few minutes! So here's the deal: In every Disney Park, on any given day, there are groups of trainees and Disney Management walking through the park and checking out the operation. Most of these groups are loaded with great pins because they just left the office! So when you see a group of Disney Cast Members pick a member of the group and start trading! Ask lots of questions, find out what they're up to, be interested and you might find yourself loaded down with pins and free stuff.

Resort Hotels each have their own unique Disney Pin Collecting opportunities. Each of the Disney Resorts in Walt Disney World even have their own pin series. For example if you like Crush from Finding Nemo, you definitely want to check out the pins from the Vera Beach Resort! Each resort also had 1 or 2 pin boards or bags for you to trade with. Make sure you check out both the Front Desk and the Gift Shops. If you are around the Disneyland Hotel in Anaheim, CA you can check out the Pin Board at the Front desk, and then pop into the small Gift Shop where young Pin Traders can trade with Donald. Check it out.

Start a conversation. All too often guests are in a hurry to trade and move on as there is so much to do and so little time to do it. However, we have found that when you take a little time to actually talk with the person you are trading with and take an interest in what they are doing or how long they have worked with Disney, good things happen. Most Cast Members have a bag of pins with them to restock their lanyards. When you take the time (1-2 minutes) to have a quick conversation, they may ask that magical question "Is there anything in particular you are looking for?" and pull out the extra inventory. We've had a lot of sets completed and received many perks (Fast Passes, Bonus Pins and even VIP Seating for Fireworks) just by being nice. When it comes right down to it, isn't getting to interact with people the real reason why you're trading pins in the first place?

Trade UP. Not the movie... the value. Anytime we are trading in the park, we will always trade a pin that we brought with us for a higher value pin or a Hidden Mickey that we don't already have. Yes, this means you should trade for the funky looking High School Musical pin even if you don't like the movies! It's also a good idea to trade for any rare character pins you may come across as they may have value to someone who collects that character. This is the rule we use when trading with Cast Members who aren't trading their personal collections. The general rule we use for trading with other Guests is Hidden Mickey for Hidden Mickey, Limited Edition for Limited Edition/Release and Rack Pin (Open Edition) for Rack Pin, so you know that neither of you is getting the sharp end of the pin!

Unique Experience Pins can pop up on Cast Lanyards so keep 'yer weather eye out for them. What's a unique experience pin? In each park there are private tours you can take (not cheap, but usually well worth the price!) and most of them come with a special pin to commemorate the occasion. Each person in the party will receive a pin, so if you are a family and you all took the tour or you all went to the event, you might not want to have a bunch of the same pin in your collection. Therefore these extras become traders! So if you want the pin from these special events and tours you can either fork out the hundreds of dollars OR you can trade for it. The last time we were in WDW, we traded for The Magical Gatherings Pin. The funny part was that friend of ours had just paid for the Gathering for their group. They paid a few hundred dollars to get the pin and a meal. We traded a $2 pin and had enough left over for as many Turkey Legs as we could eat!

Veteran Pin Traders can be a huge benefit to you when you are just starting out on your Pin Trading adventure. You can also keep an eye out for Super Traders. Yep. Super Traders. They don't wear a cape, but they do wear a vest covered in pins and have sworn to uphold the highest level of pin trading integrity. Keep in mind that these Super Heroes of the Pin Trading World are not Cast Members and may only trade with you if the pin you are trading fits the theme of their vest which might be a character or attraction. As always, be polite and respectful of the collection that they have spent years building and you will have a very pleasant experience!

 **World of Disney and Disney Stores** are the candy stores of all things Disney... including pins. World of Disney stores exist only in the Downtown Disney Districts of Anaheim and Walt Disney World, Florida. There is an Uber-Disney Store in Times Square, NY but it is not World of Disney. These locations can be great places to find unique pins and pins on sale. Check the online Disney store for big discounts on Authentic Disney pins before you head to the park. It's a great option for those who don't want to risk buying pins on eBay. World of Disney is open early and open late, so it's usually our first and last trading stop. Most of the Cast Members working in the store wear pin trading lanyards (even in NYC) so you can do a whole lot o' trading while you're shopping. Just remember to be courteous, as the store can be very busy,

 **Xtra Value can be found at Disney Outlet Stores** (okay so we cheated on the X a little bit☺) and I mean $15 pins for under $4. There are several of these locations in Florida, and pop up stores can show up anywhere... Being an outlet store the inventory is hit and miss but we've managed to do pretty well, and hey if you're just stocking up on traders, then the cheaper, the better! The Character Outlet Stores in Orlando also host their own pin trading nights , so it's yet another opportunity for you to expand you pin trading expertise and of course, your collection! Also, if you are lucky enough to know a cast member, they can get you guest pass to the Company D Store where you can purchase all kind of discounted park merchandise. If you get an invite be respectful of the areas and merchandise that are Cast Member ONLY and of course bring your traders along! As a bonus, most of the cast members at the outlets wear lanyards and are happy to trade with you.

 **Yoda, Vader, and Stormtroopers... Oh My!** For the past few years, Walt Disney World® has been the home every May to the infamous Star Wars Weekends. Well, now that Disney completely owns

the Star Wars franchise that has expanded into a year round thing at Hollywood Studios. Although it you can time it to be there for "Star Wars Day" (May the 4th), they always have some special merchandise and happenings that every Star Wars fan wouldn't want to miss out on. To paraphrase Yoda, "There is no sleep, Only Trade..."

Zero In On a Collection or Set of Characters. Figuring out what you want to collect can take a few attempts, so if you're just starting out, pick two characters you like and start there. Eventually you will get pulled into collecting Cast Lanyard (Hidden Mickey) pins but collecting by character gives you a starting point. Also, most guests at Disney start out by buying starter sets in the park that retail between $22.95 and $49.95. This means that you can easily collect an entire set from Cast Members and save yourself a lot of money. Researching for this is simple, just pop into a store and look at the inventory. Make a note of how many pins are in the set and start hunting. Your cell phone camera will also come in handy to remember what you're looking for.

Okay, that covers the A-Z of Disney Pin Trading and other than walking you step by step down Main Street pointing out every Pin Trading opportunity, you should have all the information you need to get a head start over the uneducated Disney guest.

Just remember to have fun, talk to people and share your enthusiasm for the pins you find. We realize that some of the suggestions we make (give a pin away to a child...really?) don't lend to the hardcore, cut-throat world of collecting Disneyana, but that's the point.

We go to Disney Parks to get away from all that crud, so why would we promote a "GO get that pin at all costs" philosophy. It just makes people Grumpy... Here's what I mean.

By our third trip to Disneyland, we considered ourselves pretty savvy Pin Traders. We had completed numerous sets, had some pretty cool and valuable pins in the collection, and had even begun reselling some our pins online. In other words, we were ripe to be plucked.

At specific locations throughout Downtown Disney and Disneyland, there are tables set up for more advanced pin trading. We had noticed these tables and the people trading at them before, but had generally avoided them as we didn't feel "worthy" to trade with them and quite frankly they intimidated the kids.

But on this trip we were ready. We had good pins. We had Limited Editions, Completers and Hidden Mickey Pins in volume! So as we were walking from the hotel to the park through Downtown Disney, our 11 year old daughter boldly approached a Pin Trader at the table outside of the Pin Traders Store and asked to see her pins. The lady looked her up and down and replied,

 "Honey, you couldn't possibly have anything that I would be interested in", and closed her pin bag and turned her back.

Well, my daughter was devastated and my mouth was open to say something very Un-Disney-like when the Pin Trader at the next table said,

"Don't pay any attention to her, sweetie. She hasn't had her coffee yet. I would love to see your pins."

Crisis averted! This amazing lady understood she was dealing with a child attempting to step up to the next level of something she loved and that she had an opportunity to nurture instead of criticize. She patiently walked my daughter through her pin bag and told a few stories about her favorite pins and the people she traded them with.

At the end of it, we didn't have anything she wanted, but the experience was positive and we knew to keep an eye out for the pins she was looking for. As it turned out, we found two pins that she needed to complete the 2010 "Good Set" and competed a trade later in the day.

So what's the moral of the story?

Not everyone, even at "The Happiest Place on Earth" is going to have something you want to trade for, but that doesn't give you the right to be a (insert your choice of descriptive term here) and tear down their day. And that works both ways.

We've watched guests badger the heck out of Pin Traders and fondle their precious collections like they were at the flea market, and we've seen the Pin Traders smile and politely educate them on Pin Etiquette. On the flipside, there are, unfortunately, the rude traders like the lady our daughter encountered who are only in it for the value of the pin, and that's fine. We know who we want to deal with and who we don't.

There are great trading opportunities throughout the parks where you can trade with Cast Members and learn the ropes. In Disneyland, try checking the Pin Trading Barrels outside of the Westward Ho in Frontierland. In Walt Disney World You can trade from the multitudes of Pin Boards tucked away throughout the parks.

As an addendum to the story, the Pin Trading Tables outside of the Downtown Disney Pin Traders Shops have been removed due to complaints from guest about rude and overly aggressive traders. It is unfortunate that legitimate trading opportunities are reduced due to the irresponsible actions of a few unethical traders, but as we've said with great power comes great responsibility. As an experienced pin trader you should be encouraging new traders, not cutting them down for a $12 pin! As a new pin trader, you have an opportunity to raise the bar and trade with ethics and a big smile on your face! Everything we learned in kindergarten about playing nicely in the sandbox applies!

Oh and look out for sharks...

Pin Sharks (insert theme music from Jaws or a Jimmy Buffet song)... "Pins to the left, Pins to the right and you're the only newbie in town..."

Warning! Brutal honesty alert!

A Pin Shark is a trader who preys on new pin traders and takes advantage of their naivety (just wanted to get that word in somewhere!) to increase the value of their collection. Not cool.

Here's the way a shark could potentially operate:

1. The Shark spots a potential victim – A Newbie with a shiny lanyard of newly purchased pins...
2. The Shark engages the victim in conversation and comments on their pins and how common they are...
3. The Shark falsely educates the Newbie on how valuable and rare the Shark's pins are compared to their pins, baiting the Newbie for an unequal trade.
4. The Shark lures the Newbie into trading a more rare or valuable pin (a lot of Newbies start out with $7 - $15 rack pins on their lanyards) for a common Hidden Mickey
5. The Shark may also lure the Newbie into trading multiple pins for one of their pins from the Shark's collection.

The best indicator for who is a Pin Shark is how the other Pin Traders react to them. If you see a lot of scowls or even avoidance, walk away. The Pin Traders we have met in the park tend to be a pretty close-knit group who have a lot of mutual respect for one another, so when they alienate someone, it's for good reason.

Also, be aware of "Guppies" who are children of Pin Sharks. They are pin savvy and will rook you out of your LE pins for a rack pin as fast as it takes to be amazed at their cuteness and pin trading intellect.

Yep, this is just sad.

As a Pin Trader, you can figure out which type of Trader you want to be, but being courteous, polite and professional promotes trading, where the ones who are in it for the money deter new traders from continuing to trade and ultimately hurt their ability to trade with Disney guests.

Remember how we said that there were Pin Trading locations throughout Disneyland? Well, there used to be Pin Trading locations throughout Walt Disney World as well. Now the only place that Pin Traders can set up shop is in Epcot, outside the Pin Shop and traders are restricted to one pin bag and no chairs.

Why? Because guests complained about a few overly aggressive Pin Traders who were selling pins or asking guests to purchase pins to trade for. You have to respect the rules.

Every interaction we have with anyone in a Disney park is an opportunity for us to elevate or deflate them. When we are polite and take an interest in what they do, we leave that person feeling better about themselves, about us and about their Disney experience. That one or two minutes you take just might be the highlight of their trip!

Now, let's take your pin trading to the next level...

Advanced Pin Trading!

Really... advanced pin trading? Okay, so advanced might be a stretch. Pin Trading isn't, nor should it ever be, an advanced science, but there are some things you might want to consider after you've got a few trades under your belt.

You might want to get the Pin Trading lingo down so you can sound like you know what you are talking about. The full Glossary of Terms is in the Resource Section at the end of the book.

Group Trading – Working the Park

Okay, you may have caught onto this already, but when you are more than a group of 1, you can work together to increase your effectiveness in the park. This also helps to get everything done on your "Disney To-do List" so you don't spend all day trading pins and suddenly realize you haven't done anything else!

This concept came from that first frantic trading trip to Disneyland. It didn't take long to figure out that the kids were trading over top of one another and competing for the same pins. It just wasn't healthy for fun in the park or a smart way trade, and well... goofy. So we pooled our resources and started collecting as a group.

We still traded for our own favorite character pins, but when it came to collections, we worked to collect one complete series instead of four partial sets. Of course, if we saw a cool pin that one of our group would like, we traded for that too.

Trading as a group meant two things. We now had another fun family activity (and Disney Pin collection) and we could split up and work more than one area of the park. This also meant that two of us (or sometime just me) could go get Fast Passes while the rest of the group continued trading.

Mouse Pin Trading Tip!

This mainly applies to Disneyland® since they still use the paper Fast Pass system, but if you're the one to go get everyone's Fast Passes, make sure you take some pins with you. The first time you run off without your pins is the time you will run into that pin you've been searching for forever. Unfortunately, I speak from Experience.

Communication is critical when trading as a group so you don't duplicate your trades. Make sure you have a checklist! When we started trading Disney pins, we didn't have the Mouse Pin Trading Guide book, so we used a manual checklist to keep track of our pin collections. Now with the book, we know what pins we're looking for... but you can stick with the ream of paper lists if you like!

Setting-Up Shop

When you think you're ready for it, grab a pin trading table and set up your pin bag full of traders. In California, there used to be Pin Trading tables inside Disneyland in Frontierland outside of the Westward Ho! Trading Company Store (These were actually pin trading barrels) and in Tomorrowland outside of the Little Green Men Store, but these were taken out in 2013. Now a good group of pin traders will gather in the promenade behind the turkey leg stand on the way to It's a Small World or at the tables over in Toon Town. Disneyland will also run authorized pin trading days where traders will set up on the tables outside the Plaza and of course, regular Pin Trading Nights.

In Walt Disney World, Pin Traders can display their wares outside of Pin Central in Epcot. The rule here is 1 pin bag per trader and no chairs. WDW really cracked down on the rules for trading due to Guest complaints about unscrupulous traders. Hopefully the new rules and limited space have weeded out the sharks.

Mouse Pin Trading Tip!

A few rules to trade by with the "Big Guys" are: Trade Hidden Mickey for Hidden Mickey, Never purchase a pin from the store to trade for at the request and be respectful of their collections. It is quite likely to find pins that you have been looking for from their trading tables, but just make sure it's a good deal for both parties. Like any professional, they know what is valuable and what is not, and most are willing to share their knowledge and enthusiasm for pin trading, but like Jiminy says, *"Let your conscience be your guide..."*

Also, if you're in the Orlando area, Mark Shilensky (co-author of this book) sponsors regular pin trading events just down the road from Walt Disney World. These events are a ton of fun with a great group of traders. Even if you a first time trader, plan on stopping and meet some great people with a ton of pin trading knowledge. One visit and you'll be hooked! You can find the dates on our website Event Calendar page: MousePinTrading.com/event-calendar/

Remember the whole rant on being nice to guests and upholding the etiquette of Pin Trading?

With great pin trading power...

Working the Secondary Markets

There are numerous online pin trading communities (we like ours, the Disney Pin Collectors' Society on Facebook, which you can get to by visiting PinCollectorsSociety.com). It's a

pretty cool way to expand your collection and never leave your couch.

If you leave the park and couldn't quite finish that Hidden Mickey Series or Mystery Set, you may be able to hunt it down on EBay. Some Pin Traders won't even speak the name of the online auction Giant (Like "You Know Who" in Harry Potter), but I have had a lot of success filling in sets when I know that I won't be back to the park for a while.

Finding a pin on EBay does not deliver even a smidgeon of the feeling you get when you find a "Holy Grail Pin" on a lanyard at a Disney Park, but there is some satisfaction in winning a cool pin at auction. As always, be on the lookout for fake pins.

Another great way to boost up your collection and possibly increase the value, is to pay attention to special pin release events at Disney Parks.

When there is a highly anticipated pin release or a Special Event, Disney will initiate a wristband distribution and have collectors line up. Keep in mind that not everyone in line is there for the pins, so there is no need to be concerned if you see more than 500 people in the line in front of you. Some of those fine folks will be collecting Vinylmtion Figures, Mouse Ears and other Disney collectibles for the occasion. For the official procedure on the RSP procedure, check it out in the Glossary.

The Final Trade of the Day...

Okay, I'm pretty sure that we've given you enough information to get a running start on your Disney Pin Trading Adventure! Just don't overcomplicate things. You will get excited, you will get slightly obsessed and you will spend some of your spare time online looking at pictures of cool Disney pins. It happens... and it's a great family experience.

Think about it. After you get back from most family vacations, you download the pictures, put away the souvenirs and that's the end of it until your parents or friends come over to see the slide show.

It's a memory. Which is nice, but...

When you come home with a lanyard full of Disney Pins, the first thing you do is pull out your other Disney Pins to put your collection together. Now you and your family are gathered around the kitchen table, pins glistening like pirate booty and talking about where each pin came from. By going through your pins, you relive each memory that is attached to that pin from every Disney vacation you've ever taken.

We have thousands of photos, hundreds of trinkets, framed memorabilia that we've picked up on vacation, and nothing comes close to the Disney Pins when it comes to having a really cool family moment. My kids will randomly pull out their pins and spend hours (usually when they should be doing their homework) going through the collection pin by pin.

How much is quality time between two teenagers worth in your house??

Anyhoo… I hope you have found this guide useful. The following pages are full of Pin Trading Terms, Hidden Mickey Checklists and other useful resources that will keep you up to date.

We also have a ton of information and updates on the website MousePinTrading.com and, of course, you have this book to manage your collection when you're in the park!

Just one more thing…

"Can we see your pins?"

Seriously, go to the website and register your book so you can check all the cool stuff we couldn't fit in the book!

Like the bouncy guy says… TTFN!

Pin Resources

Disney Pin Street Lingo 101

- **AC – Artist Choice Pins.** Usually identified by a single paint brush and single pencil as the logo and reads ARTIST CHOICE on the Back Stamp.

- **ACME Archives Direct** has been an official licensee of Disney for artwork for a number of years and still is a licensee for Lucas Films (Star Wars). They have an extensive collection of artwork, and now through their partnership with Hot Art Ltd. they are turning some of that artwork into pins.

- **AK – Animal Kingdom Park** located at Walt Disney World, FL. Also noted as DAK.

- **AOD – Art of Disney** Stores located throughout Disney Parks and Downtown Disney Districts. AOD stores often have guest artists who will sign and certify pins and artwork which make very cool additions to your collection.

- **AP – Annual Pass Holder** OR

- **AP – Artist Proof**. For every pin created there is a series of AP pins. The AP pins are usually the first 20-24 pins that are created during the artistic process. A copy of each pin developed is kept in the Disney Production Vault and the rest are released for sale. You can spot them by the small AP stamp on the back of the pin.

- **Articulated Pins** – have moveable parts, like arms and legs. Is it a pin or a toy or both? You decide.

- **Back Stamp** – The information on the back of every Disney pin. Information may include the Disney Logo, Copyright info, Limited Edition Size, Where the pin was made (CHINA). Most recent pins include the Disney Pin Trading Logo and the year of release. The Back Stamp may also include what collection the pin belongs to and the size of the collection (IE: Hidden Mickey 2 of 5)

- **Build-A-Pin** – The Build-A-Pin program was introduced in 2002. Guests could personalize pins bases with character add-ons. After selecting their favorite base and add on, the pin was assembled with a special machine. The Build-A-Pin program was retired in Summer 2004.

- **Chaser Pins** – Are silver or gold pins that mimic the enamel (bright colored) pins. Chaser pins can double the size of a pin series and Disney has an interesting habit of not telling anyone that Chasers have been released. Check out the "Types of Pins" section for more information.
- **Completers** – These pins are also covered in more detail in the "Types of Pins" section, but by definition, these pins "complete" a pin series or collection. Completers are most commonly found for Hidden Mickey Series, but you can also find Completers in Mystery Series, Gift With Purchase series and in Limited Edition Pin Sets. The most valuable Completer Pins are found in the low Limited Edition framed pin sets, as the only way you can purchase it is to buy the framed set… or find a lucky trade!
- **Cloisonne** – Refers to that nice, shiny hard enamel finish that gives Disney Pins their high end look. The finish is hard baked using an open flame and then buffed to give a smooth hard finish.
- **CM – Disney Cast Member**
- **Continuing the Pin Trading Tradition Pin** – Also known as a CTT pin, these annual pins were created for guest recognition by cast members. Guests may be awarded a Continuing The Pin Trading Tradition pin for demonstrating positive Disney Pin Trading etiquette and promoting Disney Pin Trading.
- **D23** – The members club that offers exclusive merchandise including pins. Launched in 2010, there is an annual D23 Exposition in Anaheim, CA where you can meet artists, Disney actors and yes, trade Pins. Worth checking out at www.D23.com
- **DA – Disney Auctions**
- **Dangle** – A pin that has an additional feature suspended from the main body by a short length of chain.
- **DCA** – Disney's California Adventure Park in Anaheim, CA
- **DCL** – Disney Cruise Line
- **DEP** – Disney's Electrical Parade
- **DGS** – Disney Gallery Store
- **DHK** – Disney Hong Kong
- **DHS** – Disney's Hollywood Studios

- **Disney Springs** – Located in Orlando, FL this is the new name for the Downtown Disney Area
- **DL** – Disneyland Park in Anaheim, CA
- **DLP** – Disneyland Paris
- **DLR** – Disneyland Resort - referring to the whole area including hotels, parks and retail.
- **DLRP** – Disneyland Resort Paris
- **Domed Pins** – Domed Pins have a clear epoxy covering or plastic layer over the top of the pin.
- **DQ – Disney Quest** – The interactive arcade in Downtown Disney, Orlando, FL – yep they have pins!
- **DS – Disney Store**
- **DSF – Disney Soda Fountain and Studio Store**, Hollywood, CA – Just GO – Eat Ice Cream, and add some Limited Edition pins to your collection. Trust us - you should go!
- **DSSH – Disney Studio Store Hollywood**, the new name for DSF.
- **DTD – Downtown Disney District** – Located in Anaheim, CA
- **DVC – Disney Vacation Club** – Make sure you stop by the booths located throughout the park, Downtown Disney and at various shopping centers throughout Orlando and Southern California (another reason to take pins wherever you go!) as they often get neglected and use pins as one way to speak with potential DVC Members.
- **Error Pins** – Not to be confused with Scrappers, these are actual Disney pins with a production error like a spelling mistake or a design error. Hey, it happens even at Disney!
- **Epcot** – is well, Epcot. We just felt bad because all the other WDW parks with long names got cool abbreviations. We just couldn't leave out the park that Figment calls home!
- **Exclusive** – A pin that is released at one location

on one date. These pins are released to commemorate anniversaries and other momentous occasions and will only be available at the location that the pin in commemorating. For example, The Disneyana Shop in Disneyland.

- **Fantasy Pin** – Sometimes naughty and kind of like fan fiction, fantasy pins are created by Disney fans and are not official Disney Pins. Beware though… some of these miniature creations can be pretty risqué… As we said in within the pages of the book, Fantasy Pins violate Disney's Copyright and Trademark, so you need to think long and hard before buying any.
- **Flipper** – Flipper pins have an additional painted area on the reverse side of the pin that can be flipped for an alternate view. It's like 2 pins in 1!
- **Flocked** – Just like a Christmas Tree, flocked means that the pin has a fuzzy surface.
- **FREE-D** – Free-D stands for Fastened Rubber Element on a pin for Extra Dimension. Pins that feature Free-D elements sometimes have discoloring issues, so look carefully before trading.
- **GSF** – Ghirardelli Soda Fountain (& Chocolate Shop)
- **GWP** – Gift With Purchase (See Type of Pins section for details)
- **HG – Holy Grail**. The pin that you just gotta have!
- **HTF** – Hard To Find
- **HHG – The Hitchhiking Ghosts**, are the most famous residents of the Haunted Mansion.
- **HM** – HM denotes either a Haunted Mansion or Hidden Mickey pin depending on the context.
- **Hot Art Ltd.** – This is an Official Licensee of Disney and create some amazing pins from their own artwork, or from some of the great pins from the artwork of ACME Archives Direct.
- **JDS – Japan Disney Store** also known as TDS (Tokyo Disney Store) operated separately from the North American Disney Stores, but their pins are tradable in DL & WDW.
- **Jerry Leigh** – Used to be a licensee of Disney for pins, but that agreement has recently ended.

- **Jumbo Pins** – Jumbo Pins are larger and often more intricately designed than a regular size pin, so the pins are more expensive that the regular size pins. These pins often come in elaborate packaging that adds to the look and presentation quality of the pin. NOTE: Check the Disney Character Outlet Stores for some deals on Jumbo Pins.
- **Junior Pins** – Are smaller versions of the original pin, or may be a unique pin series, like the Vinylmation Junior Series. Just because it's a small pin doesn't make it Junior!
- **Lanyard** – The nylon strap that hangs around your neck to display your pins or Hip Lanyard that is a nylon pouch that hangs from your belt. Both styles come in a variety of colors and of course feature your favorite Disney Characters!
- **Lanyard Medal** – The medal serves 2 purposes: it weighs your lanyard down so it doesn't flop around as much and it looks really cool and personalizes your lanyard.
- **Light Up** – You guessed it, these pins have light up features that operate when you press or turn a button. Note, these take watch batteries, so a little maintenance is required.
- **M&P – Mickey & Pal Shop** in Japan. These stores operate under licence from Disney throughout Japan and the pins occasionally show up at WDW & DL.
- **Mickey's Mystery Pin Machine** – A bit of Disney Pin History! This debuted at Mouse Gear in Epcot at WDW in late 2007. The machines were a modified Gravity Hill arcade machine that dispensed a pin regardless of outcome. The pins were part of small collections consisting of five pins each. Although the pins originally cost $5 and were distributed randomly, remaining pins were sold as GWP pins and the Machines have now disappeared.
- **MGM** – Now known as Disney's Hollywood Studios Park in WDW as MGM Studios no longer exists!
- **MK – Magic Kingdom** (WDW)
- **MNSSHP – Mickey's Not So Scary Halloween Party**
- **Mini Pins** – Are small pins that usually combine to make a set or series (like the Seven Dwarves)
- **Mint** – referring to a pin in perfect condition.

- **MSEP – Main Street Electrical Parade** (now known as Disney's Electrical Parade as DEP can at times been seen in both DCA and in MK at WDW. (just checking your acronym skills)
- **MVMCP – Mickey's Very Merry Christmas Party**
- **Mystery Pins** – also known as surprise pin that can be released at any time without advance notice.
- **Newbie** – Someone who is new to Pin Trading. We talked about this a lot in the trading section, but be nice and help educate the Newbies... we were all there once. Don't let them trade away their best pins just because they don't know any better.
- **Name Pins** - Name Pins are pins that have a name engraved on them, and may not be traded with cast members. Not to be confused with the Name Tag Series which are replicas of Disney name badges. If the pin says "Stitch" trade for it if it says "Irma" it shouldn't be there and leave it alone!
- **NBC – Nightmare Before Christmas** (fooled you didn't we?)
- **ODPT – Official Disney Pin Trading.** This is also the name of the Disney pin trading website where you will find semi up to date information on new pin releases. We say "semi up to date" as the site is hit and miss on information. The WDW and DL pin information is fairly accurate, but there is no information on there currently for DSF, HK, or DLRP. We used the acronyms just to see if you're paying attention or skipping ahead!
- **Pin Bag** – Referring to an official or homemade bag designed to display and protect your pins.
- **P.I.N.S** – Stands for "Purchase It Now Store" which is what Disney Auctions was known as before they both went away in 2004. These pins pop up online all the time and are popular with collectors.
- **POH – A Piece of History pin** (POH) from the 2005 set is considered to be one of the rarest series in Disney Pin Trading. Each pin contains a minuscule piece of a prop from a WDW attraction. The first pin in the series, the 20,000 Leagues Under the Sea pin with a sliver of a porthole, has sold for

over $275 on eBay. There have been numerous POH pin series (We have a chunk of an Autopia car from DL in our collection) and it's a cool way take home a piece of history and recycle at the same time! ☺ This series took a break for a few years, but now has made a come-back.

- o **POMH – Piece of Movie History** (pin) each of these elaborate extra-large pins includes an actual frame of film from a Disney Animated film. The pins can be very valuable if you have the right movie cell on your pin. Most of the pins feature a reasonable frame of the Disney characters from the film, but of course some are more sought after than others! Each of these pins were a limited edition of 2,000 but  was further divided among multiple scenes from the movie, so there may be only a few of the specific scene you're looking for.

- o **PT52 Pins** – are a series of 52 mystery pins that were sold in DL & WDW. The series features a wide variety of Disney Characters and no character repeats within the series. The only way to identify a PT52 pin is by the back stamp which says PT52. As an interesting twist Disney did not release list or pictures of the pins in the collection when the series released. Check them out in the Pin Lists at the back of the book.

- o **PTN/PTE – Pin Trading Nights/Pin Trading Events** are meetings of Disney Pin Traders at any of the Disney Theme Parks. The Pin Trading Events Team provides pin games and gives traders the opportunity to trade and socialize. Once in while an LE pin or Surprise Pin is released to commemorate the occasion and Disney artist often show up to sign their pin designs.

- o **Rack Pin, Open Edition or Core Pin**. – Yep, they are all one and the same. This simply means that the pins have no limit on manufacturing run and as long as they are selling, they will be available. Some of the pins that my kids "HAD TO HAVE" 7 years ago are still being sold today.

- Reveal/Conceal Pin Packs – Are boxed sets of pins that at packaged so that you can see one and the other is a surprise.
- RSP – Random Selection Process – This is straight off the Disney site. Make sure you check for updates as policy is subject to change! - The Random Selection Process is the method by which LE pins are distributed at the Pin Events. Each guest submits a form which has slots for the Limited Edition merchandise items offered. Each slot is filled in order based on pin availability. If 1000 forms were to be submitted and 50 forms had an LE 25 framed set in their first slot, the first 25 forms would be given the purchase, with the remaining 25 given the opportunity to purchase their second-slot pin. Typically, there are three rounds of the RSP process with the smaller editions being unavailable to purchase in subsequent round. RSP forms only allow a style of pin to appear once on each RSP form so that there is a better, fairer chance of each person getting one pin. (they should try this with concert tickets!)
- SET, Series or Complete Set – Are a collection of pins that have something in common and are generally offered as a numbered set (1of 10). The theme could be a character, movie, activity or the design format of the series (IE the T-Shirt series release in 2011)
- Slider – Those awesome little hamburgers… No wait. In Pin Trading, a Slider is a pin with a moving piece that slides back and forth.
- Spinner – A pin that has a section of the pin that spins 360 degrees and can be seen at all times… not to be confused with a Flipper which has 2 different sides and "Flips". Someone once told us that a flipper can spin, but a spinner cannot flip… and while we're at it, "Do you know why a Raven Is like a Writing Desk?"
- SPT or ST – Super Pin Trader or Super Trader! You can spot these amazing people by the vest they wear covered in amazing pins! I mean you can see these guys from space… or at least across the park. An SPT will trade for any pin that they do not already have on their vest, but they are not Cast Members. Sometimes the pin you are trading must be in theme with the vest (Like all Stitch Pins), but this can be a fun and informative trading experience.
- TDL – Tokyo Disneyland

- **TDS – The Disney Store**
- **TTFN** – C'mon... you have to "figger" this one out for yourself!
- **VHTF** – Like Hard to Find, but with a Very at the beginning. A popular online descriptor.
- **WDC** – The Walt Disney Company
- **WDCC – The Walt Disney Classic Collection**. These are mainly Disney sculptures, but they do have a series of pins that go out to members.
- **WDI – Walt Disney Imagineering**. The folks who make all the magic happen behind the scenes, and yes, they have their own very, very cool pins which are identified by a Sorcerers Hat backstamp.
- **WDW – Walt Disney World** – referring to the 4 main parks in Florida (Magic Kingdom, Hollywood Studios, Epcot and Animal Kingdom) plus the 2 Disney water parks (Typhoon Lagoon and Blizzard Beach) WDW Resort refers to the entire resort area including the on-site hotels, ESPN Sports Zone (or Wide World of Sports) and the Disney Springs Area. Each Disney Resort offers exclusive pins and may have a hotel series of lanyard pins at peak times during the year.
- **WOD – World of Disney**. The largest Disney stores on the planet located in Anaheim, CA and Orlando, FL. There was a WOD Store on 5th Ave in NYC, but it closed in 2009. There is now a Disney store in Time Square that offers pins unique to that location... and yes, they occasionally trade pins.
- **YOD – 100 Years of Disney Pins** which were distributed through Disney Stores in 2001. The Set contains 99 core pins plus a pin for each state.
- **YOM – Years of Magic Pins** released for Walt's 100 Years of Magic Birthday Celebration in DL & WDW in 2001.

We like it when Pins Move! A few cool examples of
Hinged and Sliding Pins, both with hidden images.

Disney Pin Checklists...

Okay, so now there are over 116,000 pins and we would love to provide a checklist for all of them, but we like the trees better as trees than as paper.

What you will find on the pages that follow are checklists for Cast Lanyard & Hidden Mickey Pins from 2003 thru the release of this edition of the book. Finding out what was included in each HM series took up a lot of time during our first two trips to Disneyland and we ended up getting wrong information and getting generally frustrated.

See, we didn't have this book! We think these are the definitive checklists and we've sorted them by collection, park, and the year they were released.

We hope you find it helpful!

OKAY! So here's the deal with the Hidden Mickey Checklists...

When Disney started the Cast Lanyard Series (now known as the Hidden Mickey series), the pins were released and sometimes re-released in subsequent years, as the collection spanned more than one year. That's why you might see the same pin on a few different lists. On top of that, Disney would release some pins from WDW in DL and some pins from DL in WDW... Did that make you feel a bit Dopey?

Us too! In fact, figuring out what pin went with what year was one of the most confusing things for us when we started pin trading, as the date on the pin didn't always match the list. Most of this "Collection Confusion" happens in 2005-2007 (for a long time we referred to 2007 as the "Year of Hidden Mickey Pins" because we thought there were so many pins released!) because the pins sort of accumulate on the list. So, let's simplify...

If you have a pin, and it shows on different lists, it's the same pin. So check it off. Just make sure that it is exactly the same pin. For example, Disney has released 4 different Monorail Sets between 2004 and 2011 and they are very similar. Also some pins were released as part of the early Cast Lanyard series without the Mickey head on the front and then re-released later with the Mickey Head.

Mouse Pin Trading Tip!

Between 2004 and 2007, Disney moved from Cast Lanyard Pins to the Hidden Mickey Cast Lanyard Pin program. This transition was far from smooth and adds major confusion for collectors. The source of the confusion is that it is possible to have 3 different variations of the same pin! Not only will you find crossover between pins released in 2004 and re-released in 2007, you will also find the same pin with a CAST LANYARD SERIES back stamp, a HIDDEN MICKEY SERIES back stamp or NO SERIES back stamp at all! And, on top of all that, there's one more variation... These pins were produced both with and without a HIDDEN MICKEY on the face of the pin! All of this confusion complicates the ability to authenticate these early pins, so before you write off a pin as a scrapper or fake, double-check. You can have 3 versions of the same pin!

Now that we've cleared that up... On to the lists!

NOTE: Some series have what are called "Completer Pins". On our checklists rather than listing them separately, we've put them with their series and highlighted them by putting a box around them, so you would know which ones are the "Completer Pins". Completer Pins are usually released after the initial series has been out for a while, so you can look for the 2015 Completer Pins sometime in 2016.

After the Cast Lanyard and Hidden Mickey Checklists, which are broken down by Theme Park and by Year or Wave, you will also find a few additional checklists that might interest you.

Here is a brief summary of what checklists are included in this edition:

- Disneyland® Cast Lanyard & Hidden Mickey Pins 2003 – 2015
- Walt Disney World® Cast Lanyard & Hidden Mickey Pins 2004 – 2015
- PT52 Series that was released in 2010
- Annual Theme Park Mystery Series 2011 – 2016

As each new edition of the book is released we update these lists and also add to them so please check for the latest edition to the book. As long as you have registered your book on our website, we send out emails to everyone when a new version is available for sale.

Disneyland® Resort Cast Lanyard Series 1 Pins (2003)

Tigger & Pooh

Chip & Dale Rescue Rangers

Surfing

California License Plates

Tinkerbell Starburst

Princess Portraits

Dopey Dwarf

Gold Indy Racers

Winnie the Pooh – Seasons

Gold Signatures

Mickey & Minnie Babies

Western Hats

Princes on Horseback

Mickey & Minnie Exclamations

Disneyland® Resort Cast Lanyard Series 2.5 Pins (2004)

UnBirthday Series

Kite Series

Princess Star Collection

Disneyland® Resort Cast Lanyard Series 3 Pins (2005)

Safari Series

Nemo Pet Shop Bags

Surfboard Series

Fab 5 Sports

Mickey & Minnie Pin Trading

Winnie the Pooh Dream Job Series

 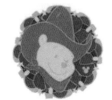  

Princess Fan Series

Tinkerbell Morning to Night Series

Mickey Ticket Series

Hatbox Series

Superhero Series

Winnie the Pooh Cloud 9 Series

Disneyland® Resort Cast Lanyard Series 4 Pins (2006)

Diamond Series

Alice in Wonderland Pocket Watch Series 1

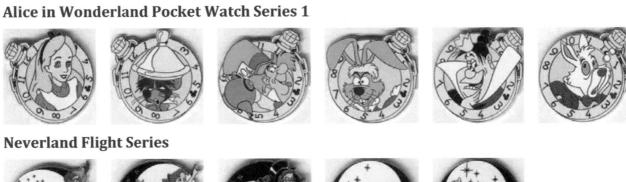

Neverland Flight Series

Beach Ball Series

Beach Pail Series

Tinker Bell & Pixie Friends Series

Royal Couple Banner Series

Pirate Quote Series

Muppets Circle Series

Villains Symbol Series

Snow Day Fun Series

Scrooge McDuck Pin Trading

Alice in Wonderland Pocket Watch Series 2

Silhouette Series 1

Dragon Series

Fairies Flower Series

Pirate Skull Series

Sword in the Stone Shield Series

Princess Cartoon Bubble Series

Chip 'N Dale Healthy Snack Series

Villain Head Series

Hitchhiking Ghost Mirror

Donald's Halloween Series

Mr. Toad's Wild Ride Cars Series

Character Snowman Series

Character Silhouette Series 2

Alice in Wonderland Chess Series

Tinker Bell Teardrop Series

Princess Gems Series

Chip 'N Dale World Traveler Series

Character Tiki Series

Patriotic Star Series

Military Heroes Series

Back to School Series

Villain Bowling Pin Series

Holiday Silhouette Series

Holiday Crystal Series

Disneyland® Resort 2009 Hidden Mickey Lanyard Pins

Robin Hood Coin Series

Small World Coin Series

Neverland Chess Series

Little Mermaid Shell Series

  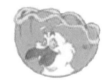 

100 Acre Wood Silhouette Series

Carousel Horses Series

Patriotic Salute Star Series

Haunted Mansion Tombstone Series

Sepia Tone Snapshot Series

Villains and Pets Series

Princess Teacup Series

Seven Dwarves Jack in the Box Series

Disneyland® Resort 2010 Hidden Mickey Lanyard Pins

Silly Symphony Series

     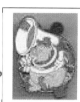

Black Cauldron Series

Character Holiday Ornament Series

Princess Hearts and Butterfly Series

Disneyland Banner Series

Aristocats Circle Series

Country Bear Jamboree Series (Shared with WDW)

Villain Mirror Series

Alice in Wonderland 10th Anniversary Pin Series

Pop Bottle Series

NBC Candy Corn Series

Bed Knobs and Broomsticks Ribbon Series

Mickey Mouse Around the World

Casey Jr. Train Series

Disneyland Icon Series

Fab 5 Portrait Series

T-Shirt Series

Alice in Wonderland Comic Series

Monorail Series 4

World of Color Fountain Series

Deebee Series

Disneyland® Resort 2012 Hidden Mickey Lanyard Pins – Wave 1

Character Faces

Undersea Band

Crests

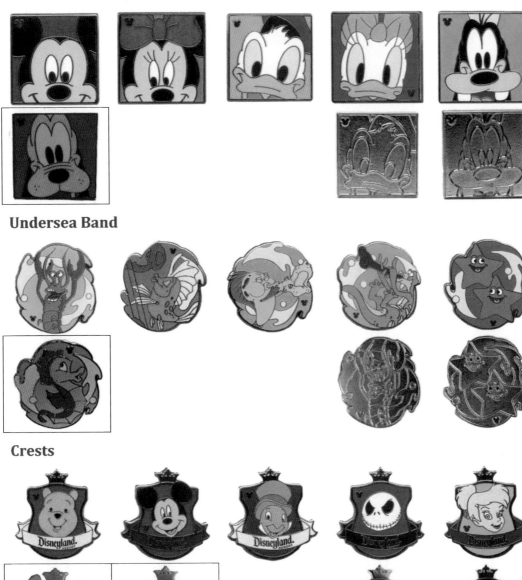

Fantasyland Icons

Zodiac Series (Shared with WDW)

Villain Coffins

Mad Tea Party

Duffy's Hats

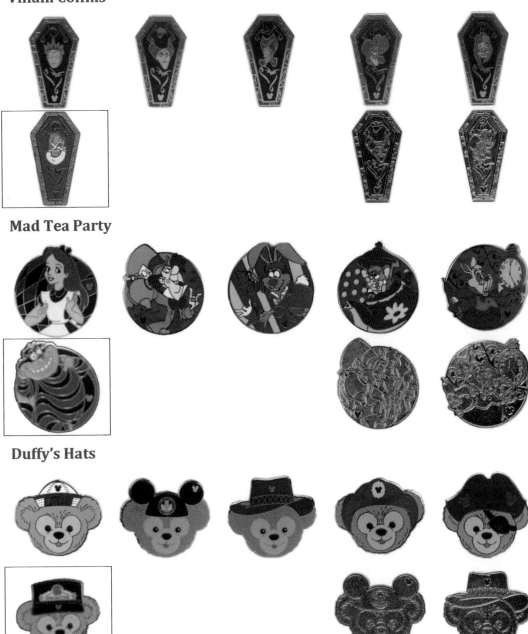

Popcorn Turners

Construction Posters

Character Popcorn Labels Series (Shared with WDW)

Mickey's Toontown Pinwheels

Alice in Wonderland Playing Card Suits

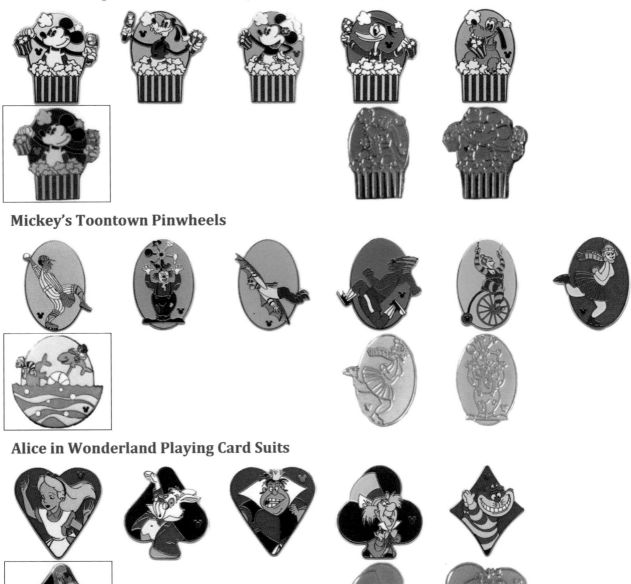

Duffy the Disney Bear in Hats

Disney California Adventure Park Redwood Creek Challenge Trail Badges

Just Got Happier

Disney Birds

Peter Pan and Friends

White Glove Silhouette

Winnie the Pooh and Friends

Disneyland® Resort 2014 Hidden Mickey Lanyard Pins – Wave 1

It's a small world (Shared with WDW)

Oswald the Lucky Rabbit Expressions

Mater's Junkyard Jamboree Signs

Tiles from Disney California Adventure® Park

Character Tiki Faces

Chalk Sketches

Disney Birds

Deck of Cards

Villainous Sidekicks

Teapots

Disney Villain Neckties (Shared with WDW)

Mickey Mouse Food Icons

Character Silhouettes

Disney Ducks

Mad Tea Party Tea Cups

Daughters of King Triton

Disneyland® Resort Diamond Celebration Attractions

Disneyland® Resort Diamond Celebration Characters

Mardi Gras Characters

Cast Lanyard & Hidden Mickey Pins from Walt Disney World®

Walt Disney World® Cast Lanyard Series 1

Mickey's Expressions

Princess' Houses

101 Dalmatians

Kooky Shapes

Smiling Faces

Mickey & Minnie Traveling

Cats

Heroes

License Plates

Movie Signs

Couples in Hearts

Formal Series

Water Park Series

Topiary Series

Fab 5 in Sunglasses

   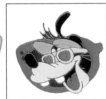

100 Acre Woods Train

Character Sayings

Red, White, and Blue (USA)

These pins have been reported through various sources to be part of the Series 1 Collection, but no official Disney list has them listed. Just to be on the safe side, we thought we would include them and let you decide.

Walt Disney World® Resort Pin Trading Lanyard Series II (2004)

Princess Hair Flip Series

Minnie Sunshine Series

100 Acre Wood Baseball Series

Grey Tone Snapshot Series

Mickey & Minnie Heart Series

Character Initial Series

Tinker Bell Flower Series

Fishing Series

Animal Sidekick Series

Jungle Book Series

Dalmatians Bark Series

Fairy Godmother Series

Pirate Coin Series

Scuba Series

Lilo & Stitch Gold Leaf Series

Villain Profile Series

Princess Banner Series

Mickey Signature Series

Muppets Name Series

Villain Cauldron Series

Resort Sports Series

Tigger Sports Series

Characters in Tropical Shirts Series

Chip 'N Dale Desserts Series

Character Parking Lot Series 1

Figment Rainbow Series

License Plate Series 1

Fast Pass Series 1

Coffee Mug Series

Figment Parking Lot Series

Huey, Dewey, & Louie Series

Monorail Series 1

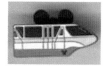   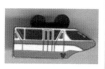 

Stitch Space Series

Pirate Icon Series

Tinker Bell Frame Series

Classic Mickey Head Series

Walt Disney World® Resort Hidden Mickey Pins (2007)

Formal Series

Character Ticket Series

Topiary Series

Disney Money Series

Hitchhiking Ghosts Series

Classic Mickey Head Series

License Plate Series 2

Monorail Series 2

Water Park Series

Villain Cauldron Series

Fairy Godmother Series

Mickey & Minnie Heart Series

Pirate Icon Series

Tinker Bell Frame Series

Scuba Series

Pirate Coin Series

Princess Banner Series

Park Transportation Series

Chip 'N Dale Dessert Series

Coffee Mug Series

Princess Mirror Series

Mickey Dream Job Series

100 Acre Wood Head & Arm Series

Wanted Poster Series

Character Ticket Series

Lightshow Series

Park Transportation Series 1

Park Transportation Series 2

Character Parking Lot Series 2

Figment Parking Lot Series 2

Hollywood Studios Parking Lot Series

Animal Kingdom Parking Lot Series

Adventureland Tiki Series

Chip 'N Dale Junk Food Series

Monorail Series 2

Huey, Duey, & Louie T-Shirt Series

Daisy's Niece Series

Hitchhiking Ghosts Series

Disney Money Series

3 Caballeros Series

WDWR Icon Series

Duffy Series

Princess Eyes Series

Muppet Name Series 2

Villains Crystal Ball Series

Donald WDW Land Series

Fast Pass Series 2

Pirates of the Caribbean Icon Series

Mickey Icon Fruit Series

Sidekick Series

Tiki in Mickey Ears Series

Puffy Cat Series

Figment Emotion Series 1

Haunted Mansion Icon Series

Monorail Series 3

Footprint Series

Pin Trading Logo Series

Chip 'N Dale Seasons Series

Tomorrowland Speedway Car Series

Car Decal Series 1 & Car Decal Series 2

Icon Series

Chip 'N Dale Aloha Series

Mickey Head Produce Series

Figment Emotion Series 2

Colorful Mickey Head Series

Park Icon Series

Character Sketch Series

     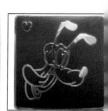

NOTE: This pin series has a blue background, not black as shown, but they do not photograph well, so even though the book is in color, we had to make these pictures black.

Fast Pass Series 3

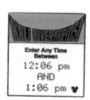   

Round Alphabet Series

Main Street Character Series

Princess Heart and Butterfly Series

Round Mickey Funky Series

Figment Symbol Series

Pin Trading Icon Series

Country Bear Jamboree Series (Shared with DLR)

WDW Banner Series

Good Series 1

Park Icon Series 2

Colorful Mickey Series

Colorful Lanyard Series

Good Series 2

Cute Yeti Series

Orange Bird Series

WDW DeeBee Series

Retro Icon Series

Classic "D" Series 1 & 2

    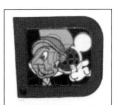

Colorful Figment Series

WDW T-Shirts Series

United Kingdom Icon Series

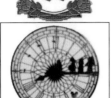

Princess Flower Series

Perfume Bottle Series

Compass Series

Continent Stamps Series

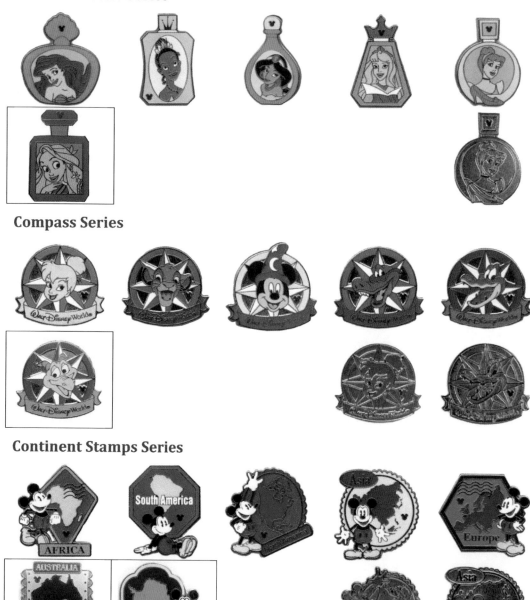

Paint Can Series

Winnie the Pooh and Friends Series

Zodiac Series (Shared with DLR)

Tonal Figment Series

Characters Sleeping Series

Duffy's Hats Series

Costume Icons Series

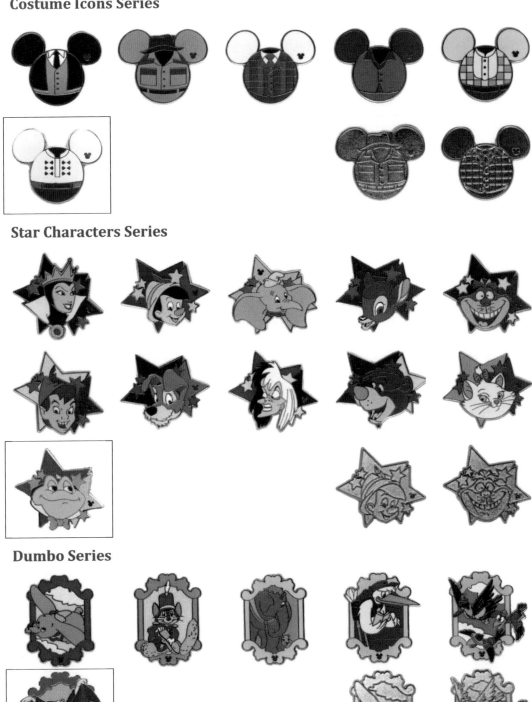

Star Characters Series

Dumbo Series

Sweet Characters Series

Magic Kingdom® Park Villains Parking Signs Series

Epcot® Park Cast Costumes Series

Friendship Boats Series

Character Popcorn Labels Series (Shared with DLR)

Duffy the Disney Bear in Hats Series 2

Patriotic Disney Characters Series

Park Icons with Disney Characters Series

Disney Birds Series

Sport Goofy Series

 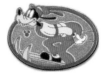  

Disney's Pin Traders Icons Series

Days of the Week Pluto Series

It's a Small World (Shared with DLR)

Magic Kingdom® Parking Signs – Heroes

Colorful Pascal

Character Sketch Pads

The Seven Dwarfs

Character MagicBands

Disney Birds

Hot Air Balloons

Villainous Sidekicks

Mobile Phones

Disney Villain Neckties (Shared with DLR)

Epcot® Logos

Cast Member Costumes

Character Sidekicks

Character Apples

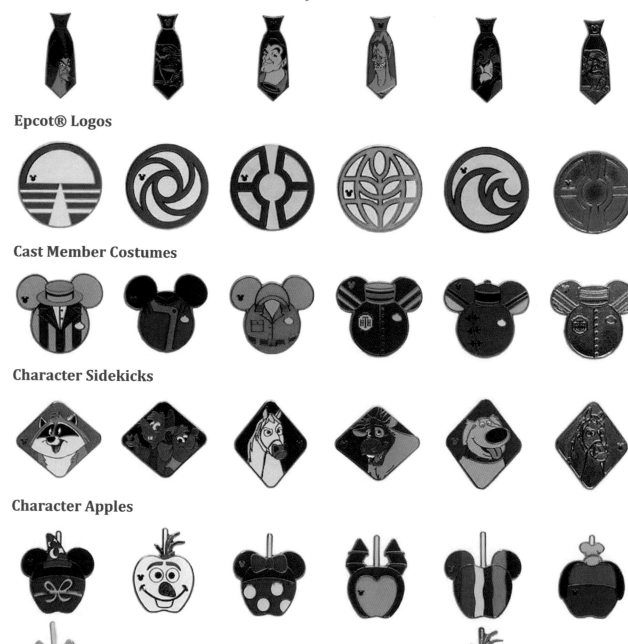

Character Ear Hats

Macaroons

Disney Dragons

Outer Space Characters

Genie from Disney's "Aladdin"

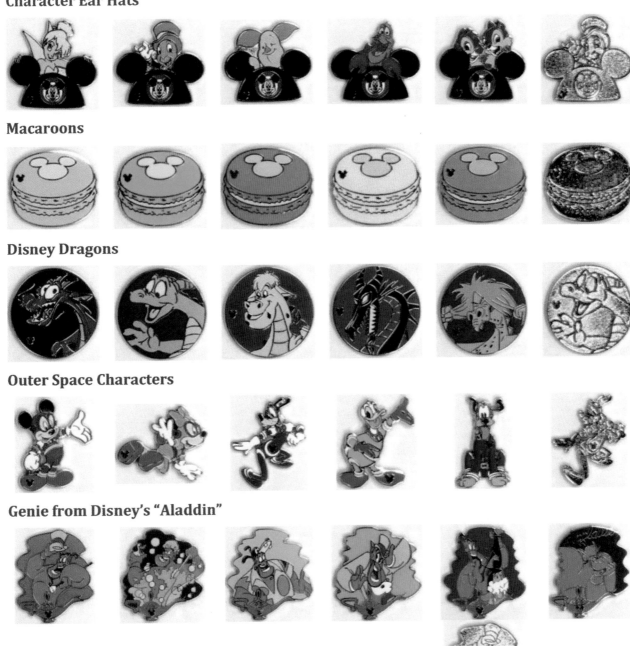

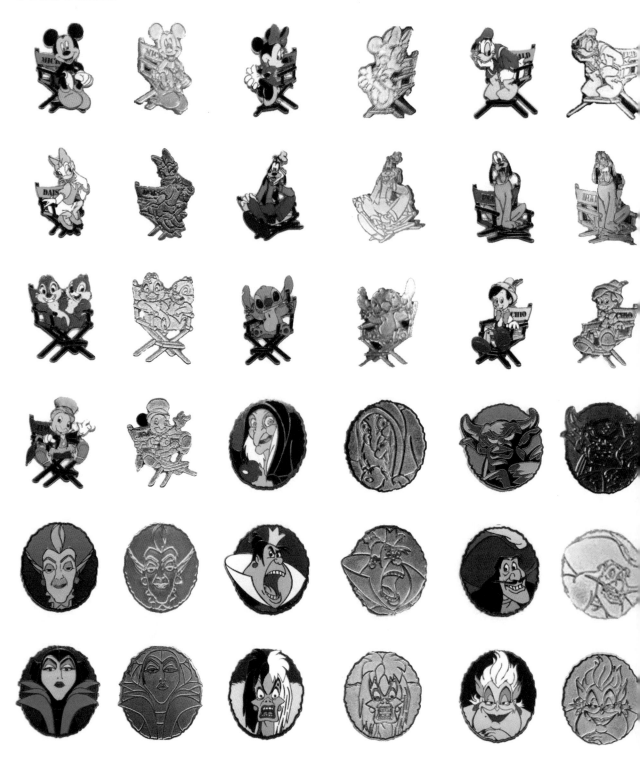

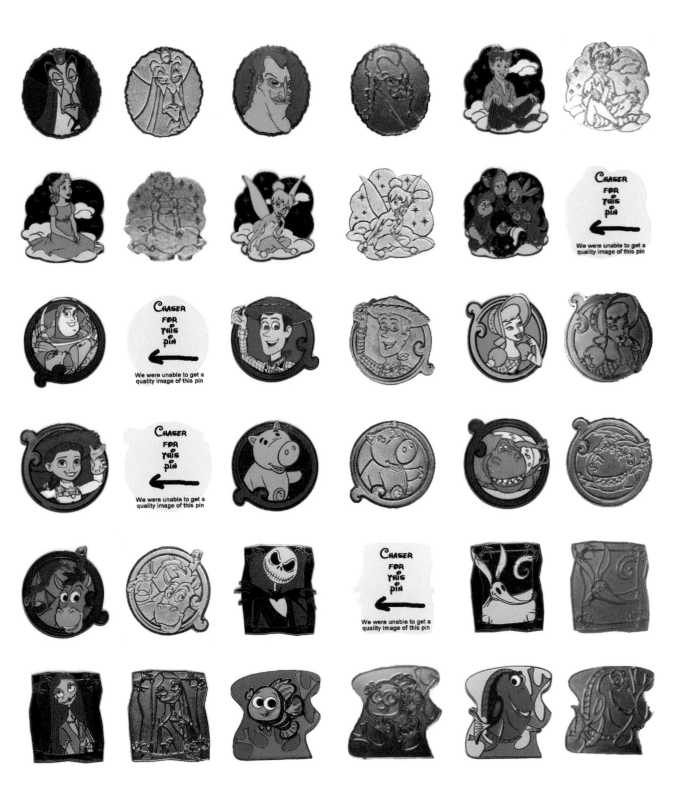

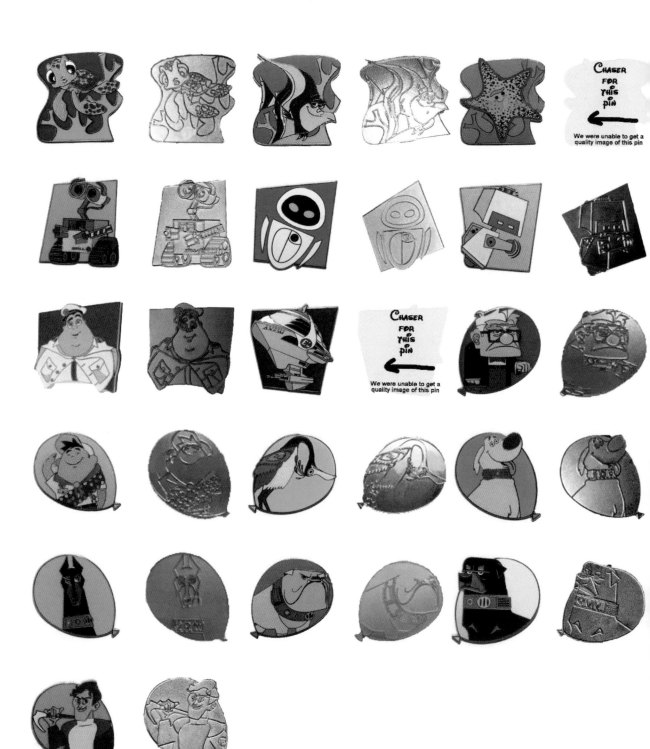

Annual Park Mystery Series

Each year at both Disneyland® and Walt Disney World® a set or series of mystery pins each released. These pins are usually in Blind Mystery Boxes where you have no idea which pin in the set you are getting. Contained within the mystery box is also a flyer that shows the complete set of pins.

Normally there is a set of Regular Pins which are "Limited Release" and a slightly different set of Chaser Pins which in the early years were also "Limited Release", but in the past few years have been "Limited Edition", so it makes the set actually very difficult to complete.

These pins are released throughout the year at both parks, but the release dates and locations aren't announced so they just pop-up usually in only 1 or 2 locations each month and when they sell out of what they have, that is it until the next month.

Unfortunately, as with many pins that are released in long series over time, after a couple of months the scrappers (counterfeits) of these pins begin to surface on eBay, and in people's trade books, so after the set has been out for a couple of months beware of purchasing these pins, unless you can get them from a reputable seller.

"Regular" Colored Limited Release Set

Limited Release "Regular" Series

Limited Release "Chaser" Series

Limited Release "Regular" Series

2014 - "Characters & Cameras" Mystery Collection

Limited Release "Regular" Series

Limited Edition "Chaser" Series

MICKEY MOUSE

Minnie Mouse

PLUTO

Goofy

Donald Duck

daisy duck

chip

dale

Captain Hook

MR SMEE

stitch

Lilo

Jafar

timon

Baloo

RALPH

Vanellope

Joe

Pinocchio

D.B.

KING LOUIE

The Beast

Clarabelle Cow

Queen of Hearts

Winnie the Pooh

TIGGER

Eeyore

Gus

dopey

Cheshire Cat

2015 - "Alphabet" Mystery Collection

Limited Release "Regular" Series

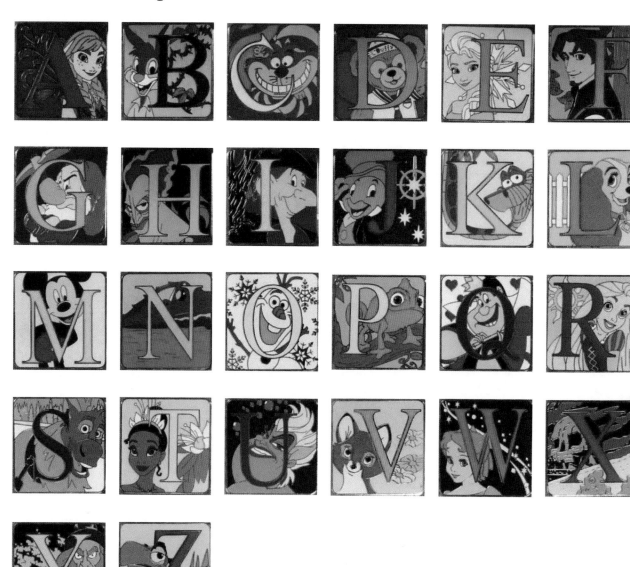

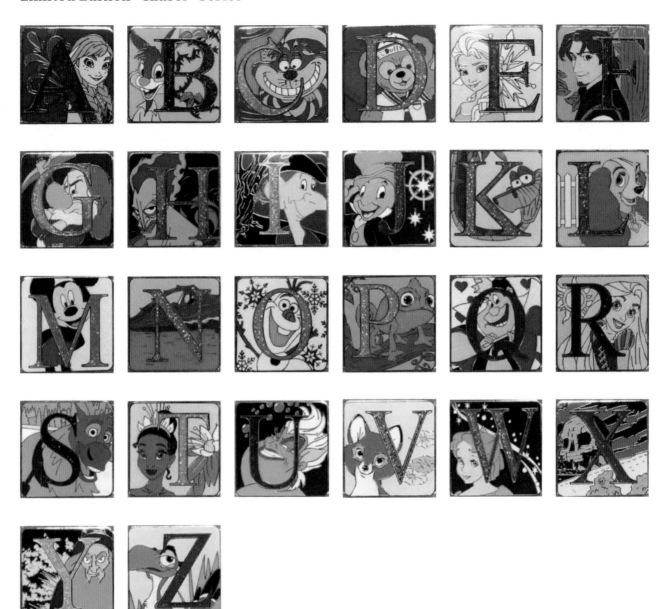

2016 - "Alphabet" Mystery Collection

Limited Release "Regular" Series

Limited Edition "Chaser" Series

Additional Resources

Places That Know Stuff About Disney Pins...

MousePinTrading.com – This is the official website for this book. If you haven' already visited the site and registered your copy of the book, please make sure to do that right now. You can also connect with us on our Official Facebook Page a Facebook.com/MousePinTrading for the latest updates. We update the Facebook page with all the latest info about releases and special events, so make sure to "Like" our page to stay up to date.

PinCollectorsSociety.com – This is the direct link to our Facebook Group, the "Disney Pin Collectors' Society". Here you can join thousands of other pin collectors and traders from all over the world to share your hobby, trade pins, and get the latest information.

OfficialDisneyPins.com – This is the official site for Disney Pin Trading, and it's a great location to find the latest pin releases, Pin Trading Events, and links to all things Disney. Most of the info here will also be available on MousePinTrading.com, as we do our best to keep you up to date.

PinPics.com – PinPics has a large catalog of Disney pins, images, and collections. As of the current update to this book, they have over 116,000 pins in their database and it is growing every day. Be sure to check the date on the information, just to make sure it's been updated recently.

DisneyPinsBlog.com – Another great resource for information that has been put together by our friend Ryan and his team. They do a great job of keeping track of pin release updates, and have their ears to the ground in all the Disney Parks Worldwide for the latest pin happenings, sometimes even before we hear about it.

MouseEars.com and **MouseSavers.com** – These sites provide general information, and are not related to Pin Trading, but ever since our very first trip to Disneyland, these are the two sites I check for deals and Disney info. After all, the more I save on hotels and food, the more pins I can buy, right?!?

Disney Pin Stores & Secret Pin Boards ...

Throughout the Disney Parks there are of course ample opportunities to shop for pins. It's Disney so that great Disney merchandise beckons to you from a retail shopping location or cart every 20 feet or so, but there are certain locations in each park that specialize in pins. There are other locations that have hidden (and not so hidden) pin trading opportunities.

In the previous editions of this book, we had included a list of all (if that's possible) of the locations that sell and trade pins within the parks, but unfortunately we realized that the list was out of date 5 minutes after we wrote it. So, while you're enjoying you time in the park look around for cast members with lanyards, ask in stores if they have a pin board, and enjoy.

Register Your Book...

We've mentioned this a few times throughout the book, and I know that there will be some of you who haven't done this yet, so here are the final instructions for registering your book.

Go to MousePinTrading.com and on the right side of the page, you'll see a banner that says "REGISTER MY BOOK". Once you click on that banner, you'll be taken to a page where you can register your copy of this book. You'll need to enter your name, email address, and if you want, your address and phone number. You'll also be able to select a username and password to access the member's only area of the website, where you will be able to print out the color versions of the checklists.

Registered Members of MousePinTrading.com get:

- Information about pin releases and updates.
- Details about upcoming special events, including possibly some local pin trading events in cities near you.
- Whatever new 'Pin'formation that we were able to find out and share, in between editions of this book.

Don't Miss Out, Register NOW, and we'll see you at the park...

My Pin Notes...

My Pin Notes...

My Pin Notes...

My Pin Notes...

Made in the USA
Lexington, KY
21 December 2016